THE GREAT LAND HUSTLE

THE GREAT LAND HUSTLE

Morton C. Paulson

HENRY REGNERY COMPANY
CHICAGO

Copyright ©1972 by Morton C. Paulson. All rights reserved.
Published by Henry Regnery Company, 114 West Illinois Street,
    Chicago, Illinois 60610
Manufactured in the United States of America
Library of Congress Catalog Card Number: 72-80936

Contents

ms 2/3/76

Introduction

REAL estate is one of the last bastions of *caveat emptor*. For reasons that will be discussed later, society has failed to deal decisively with land hustlers who flout the public interest. We all suffer the consequences.

I hope this book will help prove the need for effective controls over those who subdivide and sell rural land and that it will help demolish the myth that the masses can make money in land speculation. It just isn't so.

My interest in land hustlers began to develop about a decade ago during one of the waves of scandal that the installment land sales industry brings upon itself from time to time. In the years since I have watched with fascination — and sometimes disbelief — as land hustling became almost as much a part of contemporary America as superhighways and rock concerts.

To this day I marvel at the relentlessness with which the boondocks are subdivided and sold, at the ease with which glib salespeople hoodwink intelligent citizens, at the audacity with which corporations chop up the countryside into quarter-acre lots, and at the persistence with which the industry has thwarted meaningful regulation.

It's time to call a halt. Too many people have been swindled. Too much land has been laid waste. Too much damage has been inflicted on the environment. Too many reputable developers have been besmirched by disreputable ones.

Culpable land hustlers will deny these facts, of course. The reader may rest assured that this book will be excoriated by some of those who enrich themselves by selling land of dubious value to the multitudes and denounced by others who think that criticism of business practices is somehow unpatriotic.

Let the record show, therefore, that I am neither an enemy of free enterprise nor a champion of big government. However, I share the conviction of many that the American economic system can better be preserved by preventing its abuse. To anybody who doubts that irresponsible land hustling has become a problem of immense proportions, I say, let's look at the record.

Silver Spring, Maryland
June, 1972

THE
GREAT LAND
HUSTLE

1

Who Are the Land Hustlers?

On almost every weekday evening thousands of couples, from the eastern seaboard to Hawaii, attend free dinners given by somebody who is hawking land. Throughout most of the year newspapers across the country display enticing advertisements for land promotions, and daily the mail brings circulars, brochures, dinner invitations, and offers of vacation trips from land companies. Telephones ring incessantly with sales pitches and invitations to visit properties. Highway billboards beckon motorists to developments in the making. Armed with movie projectors and beguiling literature, suave salespeople call on families and exhort them to invest their savings in building lots as they would in bank accounts, annuities, pensions, or stocks and bonds. An estimated 750,000 persons are lured to Florida alone every year by "free vacation" gimmicks tied in with land promotions.

The mass-merchandising of lots and acreage parcels has mushroomed into a multibillion-dollar industry. "Put your money in land!" goes the siren song of the vast army of land hustlers who roam the 50 states and several foreign countries. And people respond, to put it mildly. According to the best estimates, Americans in the early 1970s were contracting each year to buy property priced at more than $5 billion — vacation or second-home lots, retirement homesites, building lots in promotional subdivisions (subdivisions in which lots are sold long before there are people around to occupy them), small tracts of unimproved "investment acreage," and other types of land sold in interstate commerce and on installment contracts.

The market for such property is so great and the profit opportunities are so alluring that some of the nation's largest and best known corporations have entered the business in recent years. "All are intrigued by the big profit potential on little equity," *Fortune* magazine has noted. For the more successful companies and their stockholders the rewards have been substantial indeed.

What about their customers — the factory workers, the schoolteachers, the physicians, the people in all walks of life who make such bonanzas possible with their monthly payments of $20, $50, or $75?

Theirs is often a different story.

Many land buyers are dealt with fairly, but far too many others are swindled, gypped, or conned into purchasing property that they don't need or don't really want; indeed many would quickly abandon their property if they knew the truth about it.

Unfortunately, most know little or nothing. The consumer revolution has not caught up with sellers of subdivided land. Despite pious pretensions to the contrary, the business of selling land has not outgrown its unsavory beginnings. The Council of Better Business Bureaus, Inc. (CBBB), places land sales abuses near the top of its list of the most prevalent deceptive practices. The White House Conference on Aging, held in December, 1971, listed reform of land sales regulations among the most urgently needed consumer-protection measures.

The conference members did so with good reason. The way in which much land is sold in this country is a national disgrace. The business practices that land hustlers are permitted to get away with are almost beyond belief. The shell game operators and snake oil peddlers who roamed the countryside a century ago were amateurs in comparison with many modern-day land sellers. "It's enough to make you gag," exclaims Anthony J. Kennedy, Jr., an attorney for the Federal Trade Commission (FTC) who spearheaded a wide-ranging investigation of the industry. Hoyt C. Duty, senior legal counsel for the California Department of Real Estate, declares that land-selling practices at several companies "have about reached the scope of a national scandal." "People are being swindled right and left," adds Bette Clemens, a CBBB official and former director of the Pennsylvania Bureau of Consumer Protection. Winton D. Woods, Jr., a University of Arizona law professor who has investigated the situation in the Southwest and drafted several reform proposals, declares: "It's a time bomb that's going to explode in a major scandal. At least a quarter of a million people have bought land in Arizona alone, and some of them paid $5,000 for lots that are actually worth $150. There's a tremendous amount of chicanery going on; the problem is just immense."

Paradoxically, such dishonest dealings are taking place in the midst of the most sweeping consumer-protection movement in history. At a time when the federal government requires advertisers to substantiate their claims, when unsafe or defective products are being banished from the marketplace, when law enforcement officials and consumer-protection agencies are moving against unfair practices, certain land companies still rake in wads of money by conning people into investing their savings in unusable swampland or desert "homesites" that may not be occupied for generations, if ever. All of this is done openly, defiantly, and, in many cases, with the full knowledge and consent of authorities who are paid to protect the public.

To be sure, schemes of this type account for only a part

of the burgeoning land sales industry. It would be grossly unfair to imply that everybody in the business is dishonest or irresponsible. A number of stable, fair-minded companies are engaged in interstate land selling, and, as we shall see, some of them have built lasting monuments in the form of pleasant, attractive communities. Yet such laudable achievements are the exception rather than the rule. The interstate land sales business is infested with a disproportionate number of crooks and con artists. At U.S. Senate hearings on land sales abuses as long ago as 1964, Robert Caro, a brilliant investigative reporter for the *Long Island Newsday,* testified:

> While it is a cliché that every industry is 90 percent legitimate and dangers are posed only by a small minority on the periphery of the industry, I do not believe this is true of the mail-order real-estate industry. The boom has been permeated to its very core by the breed of con men who travel from one field to another, looking for fertile ground to ply their deceptive hard sell.

To a large degree this is still true. Even large, diversified corporations that have expanded into land sales by acquiring established companies have found themselves in constant hot water with official agencies, and land selling remains a business in which questionable subdivision offerings are sometimes sold out before public officials find out they exist, in which some salesmen and managers make over $100,000 a year in commissions and bonuses, in which profit margins are so enormous that hundreds — even thousands — of dollars are sometimes spent to sell a single lot.

Powerhouse selling, razzle-dazzle, and legerdemain are still commonplace. Even salespeople for many of the largest and best-known land companies routinely use high pressure, pull various stunts to encourage impulse buying, and wildly exaggerate the value of homesites and acreage tracts as speculative investments. In Florida, "Visitors looking for sun and fun are practically dragooned from their hotels for 'no-expense holiday' trips to the boondocks, where they are subjected to a hammer-

and-tongs sales pitch," the *Miami Herald* said in a 1971 editorial. "Elderly people, particularly, have been known to buckle emotionally under such pressure . . . ." Better Business Bureaus and other consumer-protection organizations have for years strongly cautioned the public never to buy land in haste or without inspecting it in person and making a careful investigation. Salespeople do their best to inveigle people to defy those strictures.

The damage that results may far exceed the financial losses suffered by victimized buyers. In their helter-skelter rush for a quick buck, the more audacious companies wantonly spoil the environment and exploit valuable land resources. Just as oil companies and franchisers scramble for commercial locations, leaving the countryside strewn with bankrupt gas stations and fast-food outlets, hordes of land hustlers race to grab up and subdivide huge tracts of acreage, regardless of housing needs. Often such profligate subdividing artificially inflates prices of surrounding land, drives up taxes, causes disorderly growth patterns, and worsens housing shortages. Thus millions of people who have never had direct dealings with land companies are indirectly affected by their depredations.

The magnitude of the problem of land sales abuses is not widely known or understood. It is generally believed that most of the trouble ended with the enactment in 1968 of a federal truth-in-land-sales law. This is not the case.

It is true that the law, together with a series of other legal, regulatory, and congressional actions — including the Truth-in-Lending Act — has helped to eliminate the most blatant swindles, but it has had relatively little impact on the subtler, slicker, more insidious techniques that, in terms of dollar volume, are the most pernicious of all. Indeed, there is convincing evidence that the land sales law is aiding and abetting some unscrupulous operators; they are, in fact, now able to boast to prospective purchasers that their offerings are registered with the federal government.

In 1970, more than a year after the land sales law became operative, the *St. Petersburg Times* reported, after a lengthy investigation, that the selling of "swampland to unsuspecting northerners" still amounted to a "national scandal" that "is posing a threat to the public interest of all Floridians." The following year a team of economists, lawyers, and other investigators led by Ralph Nader, the redoubtable consumer champion, documented numerous examples of fraud, deception, shoddy development, and environmental damage in a massive study of the operations and political machinations of land interests in California. In a 500,000-word report, entitled *Power and Land in California,* the Nader task force asserted that a huge interlocking power structure governs that state's land and water resources and threatens to rob California of its basic wealth. "Land interests in California, to a significant extent, have bought, intimidated, compromised, and supplied key officials and state and local government to a point where these interests govern the governors," the report said. Developers are not the only ones involved in this problem, but they have an important role.

Also in 1971, hundreds of people who bought land from GAC Properties, Inc., the largest land company of its kind in the United States, charged in public hearings that they had been gouged, pressured, or deceived by salesmen. GAC did not deny the accusations. The company was barred from selling in one state and charged by another with using misrepresentation and false advertising.

Three subsidiaries of the Boise Cascade Corporation, the largest U.S. developer of recreation communities, were accused in suits filed by California authorities of using deceptive tactics in selling lots in California. In early 1972 the subsidiaries were charged in a contempt-of-court citation with continuing the same offenses in violation of a restraining order. In Maryland, the state real estate board ordered a 90-day suspension of sales at Boise's Ocean Pines development after finding that unlicensed personnel had been selling property there.

In 1970 California officials filed a $25 million lawsuit charging the promoters of a Baja California development with fraud, misrepresentation, and misappropriation of funds. Not long after that, a grand jury in Riverside, California, indicted two developers, a county supervisor, his campaign manager, and the county attorney on bribery charges. In Boston, Massachusetts, land promoter Charles Geotis was ordered by a U.S. District Court to cease operations permanently for failing to comply with federal disclosure requirements. In Asheville, North Carolina, a former attorney and a real estate salesman were indicted on seven counts of mail fraud for allegedly trying to sell off 60,125 acres of the Great Smoky Mountains National Park, which, of course, belongs to the U.S. government and the people.

Such cases represent only the tip of the iceberg. Because of inadequate laws, lax enforcement, or the absence of provable fraud, most errant land hustlers aren't prosecuted. In the rare cases in which fraud *is* prosecuted, the penalty is usually so light that the defendants can charge if off as a business expense and still be way ahead. The most notorious land swindle during the 1960s involved Lake Mead Rancheros, a 10,880-acre patch of Arizona desert that was advertised nationally as "Livable now . . . a new community coming to life." Actually the "homesites" were miles from water, power, and telephone facilities. Three of the promoters were convicted of mail fraud, but the stiffest sentence was a $10,000 fine and a year's imprisonment. By the time they were convicted, however, they had raked in more than $1.8 million, and the prison sentence was suspended.

Then, too, the U.S. Department of Justice was able to get a conviction in the Lake Mead Rancheros case only because the developers had published outright lies in sales material, including newspaper advertisements. By contrast, an outfit in Florida, the Firstamerica Development Corporation,* staked off a soggy square mile of the boondocks, bulldozed a few dirt

---

* Its activities are detailed in Chapter 7.

roads, advertised the property as the "Nova Industrial Park," and did a lively business selling unimproved 1¼-acre parcels as "investments." That scheme was approved by Florida authorities.

By far the largest percentage of bamboozlement in land sales results from perfectly legitimate tactics, consisting largely of outrageous baloney about land values, garnished with half-truths and delivered with pile-driving sales pressure. Other products and services are sometimes sold this way too, of course — used cars and home repairs, for examples — but the techniques work especially well with certain kinds of land because the average person knows relatively little about it. Moreover, the notion that gullible clods are the only victims is completely false. Professors, engineers, doctors, newspaper reporters, public officials, and even lawyers have been duped. Of the many older people who are persuaded to relocate in retirement communities, some encounter all sorts of unforeseen problems and disappointments, including higher living costs than they had expected.

The fraudulent practices continue largely because land hustlers have resisted effective controls in most places. At the same time they have organized themselves into a lobbying force that has consistently fought consumer-protection legislation, including some proposals for measures that would affect land sales only indirectly but that head the list of reforms sought by consumer advocates. (One of these is a bill that would allow aggrieved buyers to institute federal class-action lawsuits.)

In addition to fighting regulation some subdividers have bribed public officials, maligned critics, threatened investigators, and tried to intimidate newspapers by means of libel suits.

In some ways today's land selling is reminiscent of the securities-selling binge that preceded the stock market crash of 1929. During the 1920s stockbrokers encouraged over-speculation, and operators of "bucket shops" — dingy offices packed with telephone pitchmen — sold worthless securities to people all over the country. The parallel is depressingly valid. While there is little likelihood that land selling excesses will precipitate a depression, as did the market collapse — the volume isn't that great, and the national economy is in better shape today — thousands of people have lost hard-earned savings, and countless others probably will lose their savings in the future.

Although its origins can be traced to colonial times or before, the land sales business as it exists today began to evolve in the 1950s with the appearance of large companies that sold lots in Florida and the Southwest by mail. As their sales volume increased, the companies turned from mail-order sales to selling through licensed representatives around the country. Later they opened sales offices of their own.

Today more than 10,000 firms belong to what is known as the interstate, or installment, land sales industry, according to the reckoning of federal regulators and the American Land Development Association (ALDA), a trade group. The organizations range from one- or two-person operations to such giants as Boise Cascade, General Development Corporation, and the ITT Community Development Corporation, a subsidiary of the International Telephone & Telegraph Corporation. The industry includes the thousands of concerns that market second-home lots and other recreation property and those that sell subdivided land in Florida, the West, the Bahamas, Brazil, and other foreign nations.

Operations of the interstate land companies are fundamentally different from those of most firms specializing in construction and community development, which produce most of the nation's homes and apartments. The latter concerns make most of their money from building and selling land in planned communities to other builders. In contrast, the land companies derive the bulk of their revenues from selling lots to individuals on the installment plan. They buy large tracts of unimproved land, usually in areas in which acreage prices are low and where subdivision regulations are loose or nonexistent. Then they subdivide the property into numbered lots. The lots are sold for up to 20 times the original cost.

Some companies sell small parcels of raw land with no improvements at all, calling it "investment acreage." Usually, however, land is developed to some degree with streets, water and sewer systems, and recreation facilities such as golf courses, community centers, swimming pools, marinas, and the like. Most of the land companies also build homes, but this is invariably a secondary source of income. For the average company about 85 percent of revenues come from lot sales; the balance is derived from home building, community facilities, and operation of utilities.

The terms of sales vary, but a lot buyer will usually make a down payment representing 2-7 percent of the purchase price and will agree to pay the balance in monthly installments over 7-10 years. Interest rates can run as little as 5.75 percent annually or as high as 12 percent or more.

Some concerns sell their contracts to banks or finance companies, an arrangement known as "factoring."

Most contracts stipulate that if a buyer defaults on his payments for more than 60 days, the company can terminate the agreement and retain, as "liquidated damages," all monies previously paid. For that reason land companies seldom bother to run credit checks on customers. When such defaults occur, the companies are free to resell the land. Many installment land buyers terminate contracts, either because they can't continue to make payments or because after further reflection they decide that they don't want the land. For instance, customers of GAC Properties, Inc., quit paying on contracts totaling a fantastic $94 million, or 37 percent of the company's sales, in 1970 (GAC slashed its cancellation rate in 1971 by requiring higher down payments and instituting other selling changes, but the volume was still enormous).

Contracts also provide, as a rule, that the buyer is not to receive possession of the lot until all payments are made, and that the seller is not obligated to complete any promised improvements until that time. Selling costs are extremely high, averaging about 40 percent of the price of a lot. Sales-people at dinner parties and at property sites clear from 1-7 percent of the selling price, depending on the size of the down payment and other factors. Telephone pitchpeople get about 7.5-9 percent. Independent real estate brokers who sell for land companies are paid about 15-18.5 percent.

There is an infinite variety of installment, or interstate, land companies, but most of them fall into four general classifications:

(1) *The acreage peddlers.* This group consists primarily of smaller outfits in Florida and the West that sell small parcels of raw land — some of it underwater — for "investment." Leaders in this field include the Firstamerica Development Corporation of Hollywood, Florida, Florida Leisure Time, Inc., and Canaveral International Corporation of Miami.

(2) *The land merchandisers.* These are companies that sell large numbers of building lots with few improvements except for unpaved access roads. The largest in this category is the Horizon Corporation of Tucson, Arizona. All of Horizon's properties are in the Southwest — Arizona, Texas, and New Mexico. Another land merchandiser is the AMREP Corporation, in Ocala, Florida, which has properties in Florida and New Mexico. A recent newcomer to the field is Sangre de Cristo Ranches, Inc., a division of Forbes, Inc., publisher of *Forbes* magazine. In 1969 the corporation bought the 168,000-acre Trinchera Ranch near Fort Garland, Colorado, later put in dirt access roads, and began selling small tracts nationally.*

(3) *Vacation or second-home developers.* A nationwide boom in second-home lots began in the 1960s, and thousands of companies entered the business. They range from sellers of undeveloped campsites to builders of plush weekend re-treats with artificial lakes and recreation facilities. The Boise Cascade Corporation of Boise, Idaho, is the biggest operator in terms of total acreage under development.

---

* In 1972 Forbes was slapped with a Florida cease-and-desist order to halt solicitations in that state. Forbes had failed to register the offering.

(4) *The community builders.* This group includes General Development Corporation, Deltona Corporation, GAC Corporation, and McCulloch Oil Corporation. Their developments include Port Charlotte, Port St. Lucie, Deltona, Marco Island, Spring Hill, and Cape Coral, all in Florida; and Lake Havasu City in Arizona.

These and a few other developments like them represent the best that the industry has produced, and many have a good deal to commend them. In places such as Deltona, Port Charlotte, and Lake Havasu City, thousands of retired couples are living in seeming contentment amid attractive sun-splashed surroundings — their twilight years a whirl of golf, fishing, and social events — as a result of having paid $25 or $30 a month for a homesite years ago. Yet as will be explained in Chapter 4, the developments of interstate land companies are different in several respects from "new towns" and other large developments in which the objective is to create a fully planned, self-contained community.

Despite serious flaws in their community-building approach, and frequent criticism of land-selling methods in general, most of the major land companies have prospered. General Development's gross revenue in 1971 came to $141 million, up from $33.1 million in 1965. Horizon, which started in 1959, reported $79.7 million in sales for fiscal 1971, up from $16.5 million in 1967.

Stocks of the leading companies have frequently been stellar performers. Deltona soared from about $20 per share at the end of 1967 to $110 in the spring of 1969. Horizon jumped from $11 to $48 during the same period. General Development went from $17 to $36, and AMREP climbed from $12 to $57. The stock-price action reflects the fact that profit margins of successful companies are often far higher than those of most other kinds of business.

This brings to mind a revealing statement made by T. Rowe Price, a well-known investment counsellor and the originator of several successful mutual funds, which bear his name. In an interview published in *U.S. News & World Report* in late 1969 Price mentioned that several land company stocks had moved up smartly and that the outlook for them was still promising.

"I believe in buying both developed and undeveloped real estate," he remarked. "Some raw land can be found that in eight or ten years will be worth many times its present value per acre because of growth in population, new highways, and so on."

Q: Are you suggesting that the ordinary investor go out and buy land of this kind?

A: No, the ordinary investor doesn't have the kind of detailed knowledge to do that. He should buy stocks of companies that own land. That also gives him liquidity. If he changes his mind, he can get out.

This contention — that ordinary investors should avoid land speculation — is almost universally shared by real estate experts and investment counsellors. Yet equally clearly the land companies find plenty of customers who have never heard or don't heed the experts' advice.

In any case, unscrupulous land hustlers will prey on the public wherever laws are weak. In subsequent chapters I will attempt to show why they do so and what price they exact.

2

A Tale of Three Companies

The story of Gulf American Corporation is
the story of a dream which is being translated
into reality today . . . and of a company dedicated
to building new worlds for a better tomorrow.
— from a Gulf American advertisement

ON June 28, 1967, the *Wall Street Journal*
carried as its lead article a dispatch from Miami, Florida,
which began:

> The staff of a state regulatory agency has accused Florida's
> biggest land-development company of grossly immoral and un-
> ethical sales activities. The staff reports, though top secret,
> have prompted some hectic political maneuvering.
> Specifically, the reports accuse the company, Gulf American
> Corporation, of flagrant misrepresentation in sales of land,
> of selling lots bearing specific numbers and then switching the
> lot numbers to other land, and of concealing key information
> from the regulatory agency.

The *Journal* article went on to spell out the charges in
detail: that Gulf American was selling underwater lots to
thousands of investors, many of whom were of modest means;
that its salespeople misrepresented the value of their offerings

14

in unconscionable ways; that the company "did unlawfully breach 1,300 installment land contracts," by surreptitiously assigning lots to purchasers in areas as far as seven miles from the locations they had chosen (Gulf American had discovered salable minerals under the original property); that Gulf American had gained control over the state agency that was supposed to protect buyers of subdivided land from fraud and deception, the Florida Installment Land Sales Board (FILSB).

It was that board's investigative staff that had prepared the explosive reports, the *Journal* reported, but they had been suppressed for many months, and the board had failed to act on them.

If the accusations in the reports were true, criminal acts had been committed on a massive scale. Before long a Florida grand jury began an independent inquiry with a view toward criminal prosecution. Next, Claude R. Kirk, Jr., then governor, made the sensational announcement that a Gulf American representative had tried to "blackmail" Kirk's staff into dropping the charges by threatening to reveal certain purportedly embarrassing information about a Kirk appointee.

The charges were not dropped. Five months later a new regulatory agency ordered Gulf American to show cause why its license to do business should not be suspended or revoked. In the meantime, the publicity and resultant furor set off shock waves that reverberated from Wall Street to the Pacific Northwest. The price of Gulf American stock plunged nearly 40 percent, and Florida authorities were deluged with panicky inquiries from customers of Gulf American and other land companies. Although many land investors expressed shock and disbelief, to many people the disclosures were not surprising at all. Land sales chicanery was old stuff in Florida. Gulf American's no-holds-barred sales approach had been periodically chronicled for years, first by Florida's largest newspaper, the *Miami Herald,* and later by several national publications and a television network.

Indeed, the Gulf American story was and is one of the

most incredible episodes in the history of American business, and it provides illuminating and valuable insights into the operations of a large segment of the interstate land sales industry.

Gulf American was founded in 1957 by the brothers Leonard and Julius Rosen, neither of whom had previously been involved in land development. Leonard, the older of the two, had been hawking one thing or another since age 14, when he quit school to help his family in Baltimore. After working as a newspaper vendor and a carnival barker he formed an advertising agency with Julius in Baltimore. One day a man asked them to promote a new hair dressing he had concocted from wool fat, known as lanolin. So struck were the Rosens with the commercial possibilities of the substance that they bought the man out and took over the firm of Charles Antell. Charles Antell Formula No. 9 was soon one of the most popular products on the air waves.

In 1956 the Rosens sold their interest in Charles Antell for $2 million to B. T. Babbitt Company. Leonard suffered from an arthritic condition and was advised by a physician to spend several months in a warm climate. He headed for Miami, where he instantly perceived the vast profit potential in land promotion. "We recognized there must be a tremendous vacuum in the land sales market," he later told James Russell, financial editor of the *Miami Herald*. "Only one company, General Development, was doing any volume business." With $125,000 of their own money Leonard and Julius organized Gulf American Land Corporation (the word "land" was later dropped as the company diversified), bought a barren stretch of flatland on the Gulf Coast called Redfish Point, renamed it Cape Coral, and embarked on their announced purpose of "building new worlds for a better tomorrow."

Leonard Rosen once said, "When the history of Florida is written, the names of my brother and myself will figure in it prominently." There doesn't seem to be much doubt about that, but the memory of the Rosens might have been different had they continued to build developments like

Cape Coral; it is a livable, attractive, waterway-laced community with schools, churches, recreation and shopping facilities, wide green lawns, and spacious homes. But far more money can be made selling partly improved or unimproved land than by building communities, and long before the bulldozers stopped raising dust at Cape Coral, the Rosens were off on their next venture — Golden Gate Estates.

Spread over more than 114,000 acres of southwest Florida's Collier County, including parts of Big Cypress Swamp, Golden Gate Estates consisted of a small residential community called Golden Gate and 113,397 acres of boondocks called Golden Gate Estates. The land in Golden Gate Estates was sold in 1¼-acre tracts for "investment." All that Gulf American furnished in the way of improvements were drainage canals and dirt roads. "Buy it by the acre and sell it by the lot," went the sales spiel. Prospective buyers were shown enticing color movies of Cape Coral and told that Golden Gate Estates would develop the same way. It hasn't,* but the subdivision proved to be a real gusher, from a profit point of view.

Then, since totally unimproved lots can be more profitable than any other kind if they are merchandised "properly," River Ranch Acres was born. This 63,000-acre offering in central Florida, 19 miles east of Lake Wales, inspired Larry Birger of the *Miami News* to write:

> The Gulf American Land Corp., king of Florida's golden-tongued land salesmen, today turned to selling faith — at $800 an acre. . . . No roads. No schools. No drainage. No churches. No golf courses or country club. Just land.

Said Leonard Rosen: "We're promising nothing, absolutely nothing. We're offering what we believe to be an excellent investment at low cost and with the company's good name behind it. It will be a place where the unsophisticated investor can . . . take pleasure in his property."

---

* By the end of 1971 Golden Gate had 2,497 residents; Golden Gate Estates had none.

To attract unsophisticated investors Gulf put its corps of telephone salespeople to work and printed gaudy brochures that described the offering as "an outstanding in-the-path-of-progress investment property with a high profit potential in the foreseeable future." Letters to prospective buyers said that a purchase of River Ranch acreage "can be the first step to financial security."

The land, for which Gulf paid less than $100 an acre, was sold in 1¼-acre parcels for $800 an acre, $30 down and $30 a month, plus 6 percent interest on financing. Buyers were led to believe that the little parcels would jump in value and could be sold at a profit. Salespeople showed movies of Cape Coral, implying that the same thing could happen at River Ranch. Yet nobody knew whether the River Ranch property would ever have any practical value; large sections of it are under water, and one area is within three miles of an air force practice bombing range. Many buyers do not receive mineral rights.

To spur sales Gulf built a clubhouse, riding stable, shooting range, and a small lodge near the entrance to the property. Buyers of acreage were permitted to use these facilities — for a fee.

Gulf's next offering, Remuda Ranch Grants, was similar to River Ranch Acres. Located in South Florida, Remuda embraced 80,000 acres, 80 percent of which was under water, according to official property reports.

"It would be difficult to envision a commodity with a greater universal appeal than the type of land which Gulf American makes available to men and women of average means everywhere," the company boasted in a full-color, 16-page advertising supplement that appeared in major U.S. newspapers in 1967. In an article published in the September 2, 1967, issue of the *New Republic* John Hunter wrote of Remuda:

> The fantastic Gulf American Corp., in its most fantastic operation so far, is selling thousands of acres of water to people

who came down to Florida to buy dirt, and is doing so legally, open and aboveboard, at, so help me, $1000 an acre. Which means these people ought to be awarded some kind of Nobel Prize for salesmanship.

"I can outsell any competitor at four o'clock in the morning or at any other time," Leonard Rosen once bragged to an interviewer. His sales force came on with the subtlety of a panzer division. "The Gulf American army is everywhere — on the Florida streets and beaches soliciting tourists, in Oshkosh and Newark inviting the middle class to free dinners and Florida movies, on the telephone running up the biggest long-distance bill in the state," wrote *Miami Herald* reporter Juanita Greene in January, 1966.

To boost the sales volume even more, Gulf acquired a travel agency and a charter airline. Thousands of potential purchasers were flown to the various properties in 15 company-owned aircraft. What awaited them in Florida was described by Trevor Armbrister, who visited Golden Gate Estates while researching an article that appeared in the April 27, 1967, issue of the *Saturday Evening Post:*

> We pulled in at Gulf American's modern brick headquarters building. Outside were scores of cars, bearing license plates from Pennsylvania, Illinois, Indiana, and Ohio. Inside the prospects — many of them elderly — sat waiting for salesmen to call their numbers. With assembly-line precision company representatives steered each prospect into one of 26 tiny sales cubicles to hear the first part of the sales pitch. The nickname for the two rows of cubicles, we learned later, is the cattle chute.

Armbrister was one of several reporters who posed as interested buyers and wrote lurid accounts of what happened to them. One *Miami Herald* correspondent with a concealed tape recorder itemized more than 43 false or misleading statements that were made to him. There were innumerable complaints of salespeople's failing to furnish prospective buyers with state-approved prospectuses, as required by law.

Gulf American agents overseas ranged from London to

the Far East. American tourists were forever running into them in places such as Paris, Frankfort, and Hong Kong. In Thailand the *Bangkok Post,* an English language newspaper, reported that U.S. combat troops on rest-and-rehabilitation leave from Vietnam were being steered into hotel hospitality suites by young women posing as Florida "public relations" personnel and then sweet-talked into buying lots in Remuda Ranch Grants. "Bogged down in U.S., Gulf American Corporation Tactics Stir Resentment Here," the headline said.

Such tactics were reprehensible, but they were eminently successful. By 1967 Gulf American had become Florida's fourth largest publicly held corporation, a \$350-million empire with 500,000 acres of land in Florida and elsewhere and more than 123,000 paying customers in 60 foreign countries, several U.S. possessions, and every state in the continental United States. In 1966 the company reported an after-tax income of \$22 million from \$114 million in sales.

Had it not been for a political fluke that year, Gulf might have grown to mind-boggling dimensions.

Although its selling antics had been described by several national publications, the worst that had befallen the company in the way of official restraints was a public reprimand from the FILSB, which found in 1965 that Gulf had engaged in deceptive selling tactics. In fact, nothing changed. The Rosens had influential friends, including Haydon Burns, the former mayor of Jacksonville who ascended to the governorship in 1964. Governor Burns appointed two Gulf officials, including Leonard Rosen: and two other persons who had business connections with the company, to the five-member FILSB.* Thus Gulf American controlled the agency that was supposed to regulate it.

In the Democratic primary of 1966 Burns waged such an offensive reelection campaign (his term lasted only two years

---

* Rosen eventually resigned after ducking several invitations in 1966 to testify before a U.S. Senate banking subcommittee investigating land frauds.

author; the company wanted no more critiques like the one that had appeared in the *New Republic*.) Later, GAC said River Ranch Acres also would be phased out. But subsequent developments raised doubts about the company's assertedly good intentions. In the fall of 1971 the California Department of Real Estate filed suit for an injunction, civil penalties, and other relief against GAC Properties, Inc., and International Enterprises, Inc., of California, a GAC agent. The department accused the defendants of misrepresenting property in Rio Rico, a 55,000-acre development in Arizona that GAC inherited from Gulf American, and of soliciting sales in California without a state permit. Hoyt Duty, senior legal counsel for the department, said GAC had ignored two previous orders to cease.

In the federal court at Tucson, Arizona, three married couples filed a class action suit accusing GAC of fraud, deceit, and misrepresentation in sales of land at Rio Rico. They asked for $100 million in damages on behalf of 20,000 persons who bought property there.

In Hollywood, Florida, north of Miami, Mayor David Keating accused GAC Properties officials of threatening him and three city commissioners with "blackmail" after the city approved an ordinance limiting the number of apartments and hotel rooms that can be built on an acre of land. GAC served notice that it would sue Keating and the commissioners personally for any damages the company might suffer if it were prevented from putting between 12,000 and 18,000 apartments on a 410-acre tract it owns in Hollywood. Commented the *Miami Herald*: "We hope Mayor Keating and the commission will stand firm. If they do not, then it will be time to turn in the Hollywood city charter and give the community as a fiefdom to GAC."

State regulatory authorities in Rhode Island shut down GAC Properties' sales operations for seven weeks. The suspension was lifted in January, 1972, after GAC refunded $235,000 to 86 customers who complained of misrepresentation and other offenses by GAC. During and after a series of hearings in 1971 on GAC's sales activities in Rhode Island and Massachusetts 129 separate complaints were lodged.

GAC's difficulties in Rhode Island resulted from the defection of two of its salesmen, John R. Assalone, Jr., and Gordon Campbell. Assalone, who grew up in Coventry, Rhode Island, and had worked as a salesman for a local real estate broker, spent six months with GAC and earned $17,000 in commissions by selling property in Barefoot Bay, a recreational development on Florida's eastern coast. "I thought at first it was a pretty good thing," he said later. "But then I kept running into people who had bought property before from GAC and had been unable to sell it." When Assalone confronted GAC officials with this fact, he was invited to Florida and offered a promotion with an annual earnings potential of $70,000. He turned it down, quit, formed the Rhode Island Consumer Protection Council, Inc., filed charges of misrepresentation against GAC, and began to picket GAC's dinner parties. GAC responded with a libel suit against him. Assalone subsequently was threatened with physical violence by two "hoodlum types," who were, according to Assalone, later jailed for extortion in another matter.

At the hearings held by the Rhode Island Department of Business Regulation an overflow crowd had to be admonished several times for angry outbursts. Scores of customers testified that terms of their contracts were changed without their knowledge after they had signed them, that salespeople lied about the value of lots, that the company reneged on promises of free property-inspection trips, and that other aspects of agreements were not fulfilled.

Lorraine Bradford said that when her husband was laid off from his job, the couple had tried to meet expenses by selling a lot they had bought at Remuda Ranch Grants before sales of that property were suspended. "We were told by a real estate broker that the lot is worthless," she said. William R. Sweet charged that his signature was forged on a GAC contract. Blanche Hardy of Fall River, Massachusetts,

said that she bought two parcels at Rio Rico with the under-
standing that she would receive a full refund if she saw it
and didn't like it but that the company never came through
with an inspection trip. Anne Mansfield of Taunton, Massachusetts, said that she signed a contract for property in Barefoot Bay that stipulated that improvements there would be
completed by October, 1972, but that when a copy of the
agreement was mailed to her, the date had been changed to
December 31, 1979.

The department heard also from Thomas W. Pew, Jr.,
editor and associate publisher of the *Troy Daily News,* of
Troy, Ohio. In a series of articles published in that newspaper and reprinted by *Saturday Review* Pew reported that
selling tactics used at Rio Rico differed little from those that
had been employed by Gulf American. He quoted a former
GAC salesperson there as saying: "The most flagrant violation
of sales ethics, the most outrageous misrepresentation, is in
the time element — the speed with which the land will
appreciate in value; when GAC will develop it — really
develop it — and when it actually can be occupied. The
day of reckoning for GAC comes when the customers want
to sell. . . .They can't sell it even if they want because there
are no buyers. That's why GAC has 30 percent cancellations
on their contracts. And they sell that land again."

Assalone charged that GAC salespeople were instructed in
the use of various deceitful and pressurized selling tactics.*
"At dinner parties we were told to demand a signature on
contracts immediately after a brief sales presentation, and we
were not to give any explanation of the contract terms unless
the couple refused five requests to sign," he said.

GAC made no attempt to refute any of the charges made
at the hearings. A maneuver by the company's attorney, Peter
Kennedy, finally ended the testimony. "We don't feel there
is anything to be gained by the individuals or the state of
Rhode Island were these hearings to continue," Kennedy

---

* See Chapter 10.

said. He agreed to a consent order under which GAC would reimburse victimized purchasers in Rhode Island and would refrain from untoward practices in the future. The order was so issued, but when GAC failed to comply with it to the satisfaction of Albert B. West, director of the state's Department of Business Regulation, he ordered GAC to halt all selling activities in the state. The suspension lasted for seven weeks.

Finally, in February, 1972, the Council of Better Business Bureaus, Inc., took the unusual step of issuing a news release to media throughout the country stating that a survey of local Better Business Bureaus had turned up a "consistent pattern of complaints" against GAC that "stem largely from alleged oral misrepresentation by salesmen." The survey "additionally revealed that, in certain instances, GAC has been accused of urging purchasers to sign blank contracts to be completed by the company at a later date, offering free vacation trips which were, in fact, land promotions, and scheduling, rescheduling, and in some cases canceling promised property inspection flights so that purchasers were unable, under the terms of the contract, to exercise their refund privilege."

The only encouraging results of those acts are the changes GAC is undergoing. The company has reshuffled personnel and modified some of its operations, but most of the changes didn't come until over two years after the takeover of Gulf American. In the summer of 1971, with consumerism becoming an ever more potent force (and with GAC's sales slipping), the subsidiary replaced its president and sales manager, cut its sales force from 2,250 to 1,550, revised its sales training program, increased its volume of construction, and tightened the terms of land sales contracts, with the minimum down payment raised from 2.5 percent of the selling price to 5 percent.

These measures, together with growing competition and increasingly unfavorable publicity about GAC and land sales abuses in general, resulted in a sharp decline in sales and revenue. In 1971 the parent GAC Corporation went into the red by $56.4 million, its first loss in a 38-year history. S. Hayward Mills, president and chairman, blamed losses of the land sales subsidiary for the bulk of the setback. GAC's stock, which brought about $67 a share at the time of the merger with Gulf American, was trading for less than $9 in early 1972.

Mills and other GAC executives predicted a turnaround this year. The new president of GAC Properties, Frank M. Steffens, swears that the old ways of selling are gone forever. "In an age of consumerism those things simply cannot be allowed to continue," he told the author. "We don't feel that high pressure is necessary any longer. We feel that the caliber of our product makes razzle-dazzle unnecessary." GAC continues to sell through dinner parties, but, he added, "The parties are becoming smaller, so we can give more information to people. And we're increasing our number of home visits."

Steffens also said his company has "practically stopped" selling at River Ranch Acres and expects to stop completely before long. The author asked him if he thought that kind of an offering was fair to the public. After a long pause he replied: "Yes, I would say so. It's unimproved acreage, and it's sold as unimproved acreage."

Only time will tell whether Steffens succeeds in reforming the company. As 1972 unfolded, GAC was a long way from its predecessor's widely proclaimed objective of "building new worlds for a better tomorrow."

The third company to be considered in this chapter might be expected to have an exemplary record — except for its land-selling subsidiary and for columnist Jack Anderson's recent allegations of attempting to influence antitrust policy. In point of fact, its present land-selling activities are instructive of the present state of this art.

The International Telephone & Telegraph Corporation

(ITT) is the ninth* largest corporate business enterprise in America. With more than $7.6 billion in assets in 1971 — up from less than $1 billion a decade before — ITT ranks above such well-known giants as United States Steel Corporation, Radio Corporation of America, Shell Oil Company, and E. I. du Pont de Nemours and Company. In 1971 ITT reported $7,345,781,000 in revenues and $336,834,000 in net profits.

Much of ITT's growth has been achieved through mergers. Its acquisitions include the Sheraton Hotel chain, the Bobbs-Merrill publishing company, Morton's Frozen Foods, Continental Baking, and Hartford Fire Insurance Company (the nation's fourth largest fire insurance underwriter).

In 1969 ITT moved into land development. Teaming up with Levitt & Company, the largest American home builder, ITT purchased or optioned a 30-mile-long strip of undeveloped Florida land about equidistant between St. Augustine and Daytona Beach and gave birth to a new development, Palm Coast. Billed as the nation's largest "new town," Palm Coast covers more land area than Detroit or Philadelphia and, if fully developed, would have homesites for 750,000 people.

To build and sell the project ITT organized a new subsidiary, ITT Community Development Corporation, and named Dr. Norman Young, a behavioral psychologist and marketing expert, as its president.

In a 1970 interview with Alan Gersten of the *Miami News* Young discussed the reasons for the new venture. "We can get a 20 to 30 percent profit margin in land development, better than anything in the housing business," Gersten quoted Young as saying. "You make some money on the sale itself and additional money from interest income, which is about 7 percent annually on the unpaid balance. That income is a significant part of the profit."

Young predicted a heavy demand for lots — sales exceeding

---

*In 1971 ITT stood ninth in assets and eighth in sales, according to *Fortune* magazine's rankings.

$100 million a year by 1975 — because people want land for a second home, an investment, or both. Investors reason that the money market is sinking, and inflation keeps taking hold, the psychologist contended. "People want to put their money against the grain," Young said.

Palm Coast will probably make a lot of money for ITT and Levitt, but the payoff may be somewhat smaller than anticipated. By pure chance the project's inception coincided with a sudden awakening in Florida to the extensive amount of environmental damage that has resulted from reckless land development. In draining swampland and dredging canals for the manufacture of waterfront homesites developers have endangered vital water resources, upset food chains, killed wildlife, and created mosquito-infested mudholes.

This kind of activity magnified the effects of a 12-month drought in the early 1970s, which dried up parts of the Everglades and turned much of southern Florida into a tinderbox. Developers came under heavy attack by environmentalists, and when an ecology-minded administration under Governor Reubin Askew took over the state in 1970, applications for dredging permits began getting intense scrutiny instead of the routine approval that had been secured in the past. Nearly 400 projects from marinas to industrial plants came under review, and the state filed suits against several developers who were draining cypress swamps, charging that such work interrupts the natural flow of water through the wilderness area and disturbs food chains.

The ecological impact of a development the size of Palm Coast could be immense, but Young and his colleagues vowed to minimize it. Concern for the environment was Topic A in ITT's news releases, sales literature, and public statements. (Topic B was consumer protection.) The company claimed to have spent $1 million on engineering and environmental planning before launching its massive sales program.

The developers also set up a division of environmental design and named as its chief Dr. Stanley Dea, a former water pollution control specialist with the U.S. Department of the Interior. Palm Coast's master plan calls for a virtually pollution-free community in which housing density will be 2.5 homes per acre (less than in Beverly Hills, California). Shopping and commercial centers will be placed within walking or biking distance of most residents in order to keep down auto exhaust fumes, and industry will be, in the main, light. Factories that are permitted will have to get approval of strict pollution-abatement plans. To avoid architectural tedium home builders will be encouraged to use a variety of styles and designs. Noise pollution will be minimized by spacing residential areas away from major highways.

"It is difficult for conservation groups to argue with us because in some cases our environmental standards are tougher than theirs," Young said in 1971. That may be, but Palm Coast's planners nevertheless collided with Florida's new environmental-protection policymakers.

The development's blueprint provides for an intricate 200-mile network of canals linking up with the Intracoastal Waterway, a salt-water estuary that parallels the coastline and connects with the Atlantic Ocean (only about six miles of Palm Coast are actually on the seashore).

In giving Palm Coast a Venice-like ambience ITT simply was following the example of generations of Florida developers. Fort Lauderdale is honey-combed with man-made waterways, as are Port Charlotte, Cape Coral, and dozens of other communities. Canals increase land development profits fivefold by creating more waterfront homesites, but they can also have a traumatic effect on nature and water quality. What often happens is that oxygen-consuming algae spread through the system and kill marine life. Insecticides and lawn fertilizers add to the damage, and there is always the threat of salt-water intrusion into fresh-water supply sources.

Palm Coast's planners argued that tidal action would prevent stagnation or algae buildup, and as an extra precaution they ordered landscapers to use slow-acting fertilizers, which would not seep into the system all at once.

"Our philosophy is to emphasize the ecology of the area

and to consider the system as a whole, with full recognition that when you start doing things in one area, it will affect everything else," Young told Daniel F. O'Leary, real estate editor of the *Philadelphia Bulletin,* in 1971. "We intend to take advantage of the state of the art to which it [pollution control] has advanced today," he added.

Despite such assurances, Florida authorities called a halt to canal digging at Palm Coast after the first few miles were completed. "There is no reason to believe that this kind of system works ecologically," said Joel Kuperberg, executive director of the Florida Internal Improvement Fund, which has jurisdiction over dredge-and-fill operations. Officials became deeply skeptical of the practice of lacing heavily populated areas with artificial waterways. Kuperberg said that around Fort Lauderdale, "There is no longer any body of water fit for human contact." Arthur Marshall, chairman of the division of applied ecology at the University of Miami, said that no matter what safeguards are taken, developments like Palm Coast are certain to destroy wildlife because of their extraordinary size.

The canal-building moratorium didn't stop other development work or sales of lots at Palm Coast. If the stop order is continued in effect, parts of Palm Coast simply will have to get along without waterways, and ITT and Levitt will have to settle for smaller profit margins. Instead of getting $8,000 to $20,000 for some lots the developers would have to sell them for possibly $3,500 to $8,000. That wouldn't be too bad since the land was purchased for about $300 an acre.

Palm Coast's influence will not be limited to whatever effects it may have on ecology, however, and for that reason the program for developing and merchandising the property deserves attention. The master plan sounds fine indeed, and eventually Palm Coast may indeed resemble the picture portrayed by its newspaper advertisements: "A semitropical haven amid peaceful bays, placid fishing coves, inland streams, with tropical birds of all colors and sizes . . . sparkling waters, clean air, soft breezes, and quiet moonlit nights." On the other hand, Palm Coast could end up like many other real estate promotions: scantily settled areas dotted with overgrown vacant lots.

In any case, Palm Coast's pretensions to being a "new town" can't be justified. The term new town is used loosely by real estate salespeople because of its exciting connotations, but few developments qualify for the title. Builders of authentic new towns lay great stress on producing housing and filling it with people who will live, work, and play in the community. ITT and Levitt are willing and able to fill construction orders, but like other installment land companies, the primary objective of Palm Coast is selling lots.

Most of the lots are purchased as speculative investments by people who have no intention of living in the community; they hope instead to make money by reselling their lots at a profit. There is no certainty that they will be able to do this, of course, and the fact that dozens of other promoters are selling lots the same way in Florida will not improve their chances of finding buyers.

There is thus a very real possibility that large sections of Palm Coast will lie vacant for years, even generations. Palm Coast, in fact, is primarily a giant lot-selling operation of a type that is frequently criticized by city planners and land use experts. Nonetheless, between May, 1970, when the property first went on the market, and October, 1971, ITT took in more than $34 million from lot sales — with marketing limited to only 30 percent of the nation. Down payments average about 10 percent on lot prices ranging from $3,200 to $22,000.

ITT's sales presentations underscore the investment angle. "Put a new form of security in your investment picture . . . 10,000 square feet of land," scream bold captions on full-page newspaper ads. "If you own life insurance, stocks, mutual funds, or bonds, you owe it to yourself to investigate the long-term investment value of a Palm Coast homesite."

Prepared scripts used by speakers at Palm Coast dinner parties include this paragraph:

Tonight we will not only tell you about Florida, its growth potential, but also about what all of this can mean to you. What Florida can mean to those who are dreaming of a perfect retirement, to those who are thinking of the perfect vacation home, to those who want to live and work under ideal recreational and climatic conditions, and most important of all, to those who are seeking the best possible investment vehicle.

Like other interstate land companies, ITT makes most of its sales through dinner parties. In April, 1971, the author received an invitation to a "special preview showing" of Palm Coast. "We have asked a select group of successful people, like yourself, to have dinner with us," said an accompanying note signed by Young. "We have invited people whose opinions we value, people whose ideas can help us make our property the best development in all of Florida. . . . Naturally there is no cost or obligation on your part. . . . "

We were grateful for the opportunity to find out how the nation's ninth largest corporation sells land. I recalled that Young had had quite a lot to say about truthfulness in selling. Palm Coast salespeople "must tell it like it is, without embellishments and without arm-twisting," he had told O'Leary of the *Bulletin*. A salesperson who had sold $400,000 worth of property was fired for fibbing to customers, according to Young. In the *Miami News* interview, Young had remarked that the public had become more confident about buying land because of the new government regulations. "The best thing that happened to the land business were the state and federal laws that keep out the fly-by-nighters," he said. "If the customer knows he has consumer protection, it helps us when we try to sell land."

Indeed it does, as does ITT's status as a corporate colossus. Unfortunately for the consumer, neither the law nor ITT's size is any guarantee of fair treatment. The dinner the author attended, at the Sheraton Inn (owned by ITT) in Silver Spring, Maryland, was almost a rerun of the other such dinners I have attended. There was the same pressure-cooker atmosphere, the same sense of urgency, the same leaping up by sales-people and shouting for "holds" on property.

The day after the dinner the author persuaded an ITT receptionist to part with a blank contract and a property report. From these documents I learned: (1) a buyer wouldn't get possession of the property until 1980; (2) a sewer hookup would cost the buyer about $500 more than the cost of the lot; (3) if the sewer system wasn't ready when the buyer wanted to move in, the buyer would have to spend $350 for a septic tank in order to get a building permit; (4) if the buyer missed one payment, ITT could keep every cent paid on the contract as liquidated damages; and (5) if ITT were unable to complete the promised improvements, the buyer's money would be refunded plus 6 percent interest (the buyer would have paid 7 percent on the contract). *None of these facts was mentioned at the dinner.*

Two days later a sales counsellor telephoned to report that, luckily for me, that lot was still available. A week after that he called again. The lot was, surprisingly enough, *still* available.

I then wrote the following letter to Dr. Young, dated May 3, 1971:

> As you may know, your public relations people have con-tacted me and other members of the *Observer* staff several times with requests that we publish an article about your Florida development, Palm Coast. Recently my wife and I re-ceived an unsolicited invitation to a dinner party given by one of your sales organizations in Maryland. We attended in the guise of prospective buyers. All through the evening statements were made by some of the sales personnel that we regarded as false or deceptive. Two high-pressure salespeople tried to sell us an $8,000 lot at Palm Coast, urging us to sign contracts then and there. The dinner was followed up by two high-pressure phone calls.
>
> This, of course, could have been an unusual experience, although others have complained to us about hard-sell tactics at these dinners. Inasmuch as your company is offering many

millions of dollars worth of property for sale throughout the country and inviting individuals to put several thousand dollars each into speculative investments, I would be most grateful for any information you could give me regarding any safeguards that have been taken by your company to protect the public from sales excesses and to minimize misunderstandings. Your public relations director, Mildred Vigderhouse, tells me that you and other officials of ITT-Levitt are determined to see that the offering is presented in a fair and factual manner, and you have been quoted to this effect in news articles that she sent me.

Would you be kind enough to answer the following?

1. I understand that much or most of the selling of Palm Coast properties is done through local, independent real estate brokers or agencies who are not directly connected with ITT-Levitt. If this is the case, would you tell me how your company is able to prevent salespeople from making false or exaggerated statements, either at dinner parties or in follow-up telephone calls?

2. What qualifications do Palm Coast salespeople have as investment advisers?

3. Studies by the Urban Land Institute, a national organization that specializes in real estate research, show that land must double in value every six years on the average to justify holding it as an investment. Do you expect the value of lots in Palm Coast to double in value every six years?

4. Consumer-protection organizations such as the Council of Better Business Bureaus strongly and repeatedly advise consumers not to buy land without inspecting it personally beforehand. Do you think this is good advice? If so, would you explain why people who attend dinner parties held by your sales organizations are urged to sign contracts on the spot?

5. What percentage of the people who buy lots at Palm Coast sign contracts without, or before, personally inspecting the property?

6. Under federal law, people who invest in securities must be told in writing all material facts about the offering, including risk factors. People who invest in land such as that offered by Palm Coast are also supposed to receive the benefit of full disclosure, although the implementation of the federal land sales law has not been as forceful as that of the securities

regulations. Nevertheless, do you believe that, in fairness to Palm Coast investors, all risk factors should be disclosed in writing? Would you be willing to include in the prospectus, or offering statement, such statements as these: The company does not agree, or at this time intend, to repurchase lots from purchasers. There is no assurance that it will be possible to resell a particular lot within a reasonably short period of time, or that the owner will be able to recover his equity. The developer intends to offer for sale some 100,000 acres over a period of several years and therefore will be in competition with any purchasers who attempt to resell lots during that period. The market for Palm Coast lots could be adversely affected by a number of factors, including a downturn in the economy, a possible oversupply of Florida building lots, and competition from other developers.

7. Why haven't New York state authorities approved the Palm Coast property for sale to New York residents? Are you authorized to offer the property to California residents?

8. Do you care to comment on the fact that many consumer-protection authorities, including a vice-president of the Council of Better Business Bureaus, advise small investors against buying lots as speculative investments?

9. ITT-Levitt says that Palm Coast will occupy an area of at least 100,000 acres, or approximately 156 square miles. This is larger than Philadelphia and considerably larger than any city in Florida. What leads you to believe that a community of this size can be successfully developed and populated in what is now a rural, unindustrialized part of the state?

I will greatly appreciate your replies to these questions, together with any other information you may wish to provide.

A few days later I received the following reply:

It is indeed regrettable that the Palm Coast salesmen with whom you met were deceptive and excessively high pressure in their approach to you. I hope you will be kind enough to send me their names for further action.

I have been quoted and I will state to you unequivocally that we have had an enormous turnover of salesmen in our business. We cannot and will not have in our sales force the kind of people you describe. Our own surveillance techniques (tape recorders and "hypothetical" customers) spot many. Responses like yours point up others. For this I thank you indeed for your note.

Each of your questions, to my mind, is incisive and bears detailed response. Because I am anxious for you to know our answers and I do not want to make them merely some typed paragraphs, I would prefer to meet you head-to-head and review some of your points with you. Because some of your points concern the issue of environment, I will have with me Dr. Stanley Dea, our Director of Ecology.

I am leaving for Europe today. My secretary will call you to make an appointment after my return at your convenience— either at Silver Spring, New York, or at Palm Coast if you like, since that would answer many questions.

I look forward to seeing you.

A few weeks later Young and I met for lunch in Washington. With him were Dea and Mildred Vigderhouse, Palm Coast's public relations director.

Replying to questions, Dr. Young reeled off some interesting sales statistics. The ratio of sales to sales pitches was between 10 and 20 percent, considered a "very good conversion rate." About 35 percent of the price of the lot represented promotional costs, including sales commissions. Salespeople earned up to $40,000 a year. "Usually if a fellow isn't averaging $15,000 we won't keep him very long."

"Aren't salespeople more likely to bend the truth when they're under such pressure to perform?" I asked.

"At Palm Coast, we have so much going for us that a salesman has to be *crazy* to bend the truth," Dr. Young asserted. "We have — let me tell you about Palm Coast. . . ." And for the next ten minutes he did.

Is it fair to urge people to sign contracts before they leave a dinner?

"Well, I think it's fair in the sense that the individual has complete freedom at any time to say he'd like to take the contract with him, to see his attorney with it, and come back to the office or not come back if the attorney disagrees."

What about the warnings of consumer-protection authorities against buying land sight unseen?

"The individual again is his own free agent. We are making statements to him that are accurate; we show movies that are accurate; we show photographs that are accurate; we give them an offering statement that accurately indicates what is there. The individual can put down his down payment, always knowing that he can go look at that land and get his money back. Many people buy stock without seeing the companies, knowing the company, but they don't have a chance to get their money back."

Young said that salespeople are "monitored" by dinner guests who pose as customers to make sure they stick to the facts. "How do you monitor a salesperson who calls on the phone or visits a prospect's home?" I asked.

"Well, monitoring is on a sampling basis. We can't monitor every single transaction . . . but eventually every single salesman is monitored."

Are salespeople permitted to talk about leverage?

"Well, this isn't accentuated. It may come up, but it's very rare. If you'll read our ads . . . you'll see it's described as a long-term investment. It's not for in-and-outers."

"Yes," I said, "and there seems to be a contradiction there. If it's a long-term investment, a buyer couldn't very well apply leverage."

"I know that, and that's why we don't talk about leverage."

Did he agree that investing in a Palm Coast lot involved a certain amount of risk?

"Well, almost any investment involves risk," said Young.

Should prospective buyers be informed of the risks?

"To my mind," Young retorted, "it would be a big plus for this business if all of us in the land sales business were to have to make some of the statements you suggested [in my letter to Young]. I believe the healthiest thing in this business . . . is regulation. If the authorities put in those caveats, we would welcome them."

"What would be your objection to including the caveats without official compulsion?"

"Because when individuals compare our offering with another, they might feel that for some reason we were constrained to say something that all the others were not."

I mentioned to Young that numerous investment specialists counsel against speculating in subdivision lots. "Does ITT, with its considerable resources and research facilities, have any evidence that many people who invest in Florida lots make money?"

"No, it isn't that easy . . . even if we went out and did that [gathered information on how lot buyers have made out in the past], we wouldn't be allowed to use it."

"But you say in your ads that raw land in Florida has risen 78 percent since 1964."

"Yes, we can do that. But we can't say that this will happen in the future."

"Isn't it misleading to compare raw land with subdivision lots?"

"I can't agree with you."

"Wouldn't ITT have a powerful sales argument if it could show, from public records of actual transactions, that large numbers of people have made money by speculating on subdivision lots?"

"It's an interesting point. I'd like to investigate it. I'm a research nut."

At this point Young looked at his watch and announced that he had to catch a plane. We shook hands and parted company. Five months later, in November, 1971, the author attended another Palm Coast dinner. Our "land counsellors" this time were a couple. The wife confided to my wife that they were moonlighting as ITT employees; they operate a medical laboratory in Silver Spring, Maryland, she said, but business was slow at the moment. The husband was new at land selling, but the wife had done it before — for GAC.

The sales spiel was similar to the one we had gotten earlier in the year, except that this time there was no mention of leverage. Nor was there any mention of Palm Coast's difficulties with Florida environmental authorities.

Midway through the pitch our counsellors asked us to look at a large wall map of Palm Coast. Nearby was a table stacked with what looked like Palm Coast information kits. I casually picked one up and leafed through it. Inside were a contract, a property report, a site map, a list of restrictive covenants, and other papers. Suddenly a small furor broke out. "How did he get that?" a salesperson gasped. The speaker rushed over and relieved me of it. "Isn't that a sales brochure?" I asked innocently. "No, that's an allotment kit," rasped the sales manager, slightly ruffled but able to manage a smile. Allotment kits are given to buyers of lots *after* they sign a contract and hand over the down payment.

For several months prior to that dinner classified ads offering Palm Coast property had been appearing in Washington newspapers with some regularity. The ads were run by individuals who had bought lots and were trying to resell them. Many of the ads included such phrases as "sacrifice," "big discount," or "save money." Out of curiosity I called several of the phone numbers listed.

"I'll let you have mine at a $500 loss," a woman in Arlington, Virginia, told me. A man in Bethesda, Maryland, said I could take over his payments and save $700.

Another Maryland advertiser was trying to sell a waterfront lot similar to the ones we were offered at the dinners. His price was $8,000, but he needed $3,500 cash. He hinted that he'd take less.

"If you know anyone else who wants one of these lots, I have a friend who is trying to sell one," he said rather plaintively.

I asked him what sort of work he did.

"I'm in real estate."

"And you bought a lot at Palm Coast?"

"Well, I used to work for them. It looked pretty good. I sold $186,000 worth of property the first month."

A great deal of real estate is sold with hoopla and high pressure, but it is difficult to understand how such tactics make the world "a better place to live in."

3

The Big Sell —
Then and Now

T$_{HE}$ selling antics of today's land hustlers can be better understood if placed in historical perspective. Land, or at least certain forms of land, has been a hard-sell commodity for centuries. With the possible exception of evangelistic religion, nothing inspires more selling exuberance than land.

In an article tracing the performance of several land company stocks Wyndham Robertson of *Fortune* magazine remarked in 1969: "Aside from land, the industry's primary asset is a talent for selling." And an extraordinary talent it is. The industry was built on sales, not on any spectacular feats of community building or on any overwhelming need for its products. Without aggressive selling the industry would not long endure in its present form.

Selling is an indispensable function in a free economy. Too often, however, what passes for a hard sell is in reality bamboozlement. To understand why it is necessary to under-

44

stand the nature of land. No two pieces of land are quite alike; differences in such features as location, topography, soil composition, and zoning make each lot, tract, or parcel unique, thus giving a salesperson a perfect springboard. Even more exciting to a salesperson is land's role as a store of value, with a potential for appreciation. A parcel's present value may be hard to determine, and its future value is, of course, unknown. So land selling is made to order for con artists. A person selling brushes, vacuum cleaners, or snowmobiles may rhapsodize to the rafters, but customers are likely to be familiar enough with the product and its market value to catch the seller in any outlandish fibs. But a person who sells land has more leeway. Who knows what wondrous things may happen to a hunk of Mother Earth? Very often what is really being sold is hope.

It was hope that brought millions of immigrants to America's shores, and more than a few of them were lured by land hustlers. As will be noted in Chapter 4, land promotion flourished in this country long before the first shots were fired at Lexington and Concord. The lure of the land fueled America's western migration, and promoters were out in force then too. "As early as 1870, land promoters were luring immigrants from Russia, Germany, and other countries [to the western states] with promises of rich farm lands, stoutly built cabins, and other blandishments which often were found to be nonexistent," said W. Dan Bell, president and general manager of the Denver Area Better Business Bureau, in testimony before a U.S. Senate subcommittee in 1964. "Land speculation was rampant during the Gold Rush, fabulous sums being paid for urban sites in once-booming areas that are now just ghost towns."

Land promoters left many a ghost town in California. "Even today, 75 years later, when population pressures and suburbanization are beginning to reach some of the ghost town areas, it is difficult to develop the tax-deeded acreage because of the scattered ownership of the lots that were sold," said Herbert E. Wenig, California's assistant attorney-general.

But the most incredible of all the great promotional binges of the past was the Florida land boom that occurred between 1924 and 1926. In retrospect the boom seems almost too bizarre to have happened; it was one of those strange spasms of speculative madness that occasionally seizes mankind. Others were the California Gold Rush of 1849, the stock market mania of 1928 and 1929, and the Holland tulip craze of the seventeenth century, during which prices of tulip bulbs rose to astronomical levels and then collapsed, putting thousands of investors in the poorhouse.

Nobody was ever sure exactly when the Florida orgy began. Its causes aren't altogether clear either, although many of them are known. Times were good, the economy having moved smartly upward in the aftermath of World War I. Already there were stirrings of discontent with urban life. To millions of frigid northerners packed into dirty, noisy, crowded cities, with their ugly factories and smokestacks, the appeal of Florida's sunny vistas was overpowering.

Before 1924 the selling of real estate in Florida was a relatively inconsequential activity, usually carried on as a sideline by insurance salespeople. Then, imperceptively at first, "a strange, inexplicable, and almost electric current began to run through Florida," wrote author Robert Wilder in his absorbing novel, *The Sea and the Stars*. On a stretch of pine-studded flatlands outside of Miami an intrepid, imaginative business executive named George Merrick, a clergyman's son who had inherited 200 acres of land, undertook the creation of a new community, the equal of which had never before been seen in America.

After taking an option on 3,000 more acres Merrick prepared lavish brochures, depicting a city of elegant homes styled in Spanish and Italian architecture. The pamphlets showed blue waterways joining Biscayne Bay, wide boulevards illuminated by ornamental light standards and lined with tall, swaying palms, sweeping green lawns with bright-colored foliage, and snow white beaches. A gifted promoter, Merrick hired William Jennings Bryan, the golden-tongued orator and thrice-defeated presidential candidate, to extol the project (for $50,000 a year in fees) from a floating platform in a lagoon, and he hired author Rex Beach to write a promotional tract. Bandleader Paul Whiteman played "When the Moon Shines on Coral Gables" and other lilting tunes at the Venetian Pool.

In the first six months of the sales campaign Merrick sold $150 million worth of lots. The response flabbergasted just about everyone, including Merrick. He added 7,000 acres to his holdings, expanded the sales force to 3,000 persons, and bought 76 buses to transport prospects from all over the United States. Merrick was no flim-flam man. The community — Coral Gables — was built to his specifications, and it became the prototype of the quality subdivision in Florida. Tourists, whose mobility was vastly increased by Henry Ford's invention, flocked there by the thousands to look and buy. Coral Gables became nationally famous.

But the success of Coral Gables was nothing compared to what followed. Northward from Coral Gables the boom fever spread. Hundreds of subdivisions appeared throughout the state — in the pine forests adjacent to coastal cities, in the central ridge country, in the Everglades, and in other swamps. Most of them were jerry-built affairs, consisting of little more than an imposing entrance archway and signs bearing names of streets to be built "later." People bought anyway. "People would buy anything, and everything was for sale at a price," one observer reported. The speculative hysteria infiltrated the North. In 1925 alone an estimated 2.5 million people poured into Florida. Land prices doubled, tripled, quadrupled, and continued to soar to fantastic heights.

It has been estimated that in Florida during the boom the numbers of lots that were subdivided was sufficient to house the entire population of the United States. There were enough lots for 2 million people within 10 miles of Miami (the area's population in 1970 was 1,259,176). But many of the "homesites" couldn't have housed anybody, except perhaps in a houseboat. It was during the 1920s boom that the selling of underwater real estate became a racket of major proportions. Frauds were uncovered with such regularity that swamp selling became a national joke. Vaudeville commedians used gags about it, and newspapers displayed cartoons showing people in diving gear holding deeds to their land.

The orgy of lot selling produced comparatively little construction, although contractors did a lively business in putting up street signs and building the ornate brick or stucco arches that marked the entrances of many developments. Streets, sidewalks, lights, sewage disposal facilities, and water lines would come "later," according to the usual refrain. Developers were too busy hawking lots to bother with such mundane features.

Thousands of small investors gambled hard-earned savings on Florida property, and no doubt many of them were influenced by the ringing assurances that flowed from public figures of that day, among whom, besides Bryan, the Great Commoner, were Florida Governor John W. Martin, T. Coleman du Pont, J. C. Penney, and others of the business élite.

The first signs of trouble appeared in late 1925 when, in scattered areas, land was dumped on the market at distress prices. That same year the railroads had to undertake emergency track repairs because of heavy wear that resulted from the sharply increased traffic. Embargos were clamped on shipments, and contractors were unable to get desperately needed building materials. A damper on land speculating came in December, 1925, in the form of an Internal Revenue Service ruling that notes on real estate deals would thereafter be considered as taxable cash. The National Better Business Bureau, Inc., opened an investigation of fraudulent land sales.

In 1926 a cataclysmic hurricane swept across south Florida, inundating much of Miami, taking 415 lives, destroying thousands of homes, and causing $76 million in damage in the Miami area alone. The boom ended, and with it ended the dreams and savings of uncounted thousands of investors.

The land fever remained quiescent for more than a quarter

century, held in check at first by the stock market crash of 1929, then by the Great Depression of the 1930s, and finally by World War II. In the 1950s came a new outbreak — a second Florida land boom. Once again the nation was basking in postwar prosperity, and a new, larger, and more mobile generation of northerners felt the restless urge to flee from urban misery to warm-weather contentment.

In many ways the second Florida land boom was more remarkable than the first; certainly it was more pervasive. Too big to be contained by the Sunshine State, it spilled westward beyond its borders, and finally it spread across the country with the proliferation of leisure-time developments.

Today's installment land industry is a product and an extension of that boom. In the 1920s most of the wheeling and dealing was done by individuals or syndicates who were able to get financing from banks or other sources. By contrast, in the 1950s, giant corporations got into the business and raised operating money by selling shares of stock to the public. The decade saw the birth of most of the major companies that sell land on installment terms — General Development Corporation, the Gulf American Corporation, the Deltona Corporation, Arvida Corporation, Horizon Corporation, AMREP Corporation, and innumerable less known concerns. Because of modern communications and mass-marketing techniques it wasn't necessary for them to wait for tourists to flock to their sales offices. Instead they formed global sales organizations that canvassed the United States and many foreign countries.

The second boom had more substance than the first, but it too produced an abundance of swindles, thinly financed projects, and disappointments. Many planned developments bombed out during that era or fell far short of the awesome magnificence depicted in the sales literature.

The list of casualties included Indian Lake Estates, billed as "Florida's finest golf and country club community" (financed with $12 million from the pension fund of the Teamsters Union); Apollo Beach, on the bayfront 12 miles south of

Tampa, which bogged down in a financing morass; Harbour Heights, on the Peace River near Punta Gorda, which fell upon hard times when the Charlotte County Land & Title Company went into receivership; and Rocket City, between Orlando and Cape Kennedy, which fizzled in a blaze of fraud indictments.

Other huge undertakings fared better. If some of them weren't models of planning excellence, they at least took hold and grew. These included General Development Corporation's Port Charlotte, Port Malabar, Port St. Lucie, and several smaller communities; Gulf American's Cape Coral; and Deltona Corporation's Marco Island, Deltona, and Spring Hill.

The mass-selling of swampland, muck pockets, lake bottoms, desert wastes, jungles, mesas, mountainsides, and gulches mushroomed into a multimillion-dollar industry, but, as we shall see in Chapter 6, authorities pronounced such sales legal as long as buyers were informed of the physical nature of the property.

"The second Florida land boom is more of an emotional experience than a business operation," wrote Haines Colbert, a reporter for the *Miami Herald,* after an extended tour of the state in 1964. "It's fascinating, inspiring, and depressing. . . .The boom is a bright new city, swarming with workmen. . . .Down the road the new boom has left a ghost town. Riding along its wide, deteriorating avenues is an eerie experience. There are scattered homes, but not a person in sight. A quarter of a million dollars' worth of mercury vapor street lights are dark at night because no one will pay the $2,200 a month it costs to operate them. . . .

"You see city sites dwarfing Miami in area — larger, as the salesmen point out, than Detroit; larger than Manhattan Island. They're part of the boom, but there's much more. The platbooks and tax records in the courthouses reveal the hopes of buyers and sellers of hundreds of thousands of additional acres. 'You don't even know anybody's doing anything with a lot of property until the deeds start coming in to be recorded,' says a clerk. 'All of a sudden, you find out that a big hunk of land has been sold off to people — most of them servicemen — in Germany and Japan and about every other country you can think of.' "

Using state subdivision records Colbert calculated that the amount of subdivided land then on the market, together with what had been sold since the new boom began, would provide space for about 5 million people, approximately the equivalent of Florida's entire population in 1964.

A similar situation began to develop in parts of the West. By the mid-1950s Florida had become so heavily populated with land hustlers that a search was on for new worlds to subdivide. A few developers settled on Hawaii, the Bahamas, and some of the Caribbean islands. Others opted for Oregon, California, Nevada, Arizona, Utah, Colorado, and New Mexico. Before anyone realized what was happening, thousands of subdivisions sprung up from desert floors, mountain slopes, mesas, dry gulches, and former cattle ranges.

The great Southwest, with its wide open spaces, was particularly attractive to the new wave of subdividers. Like Florida, the area has a mild, sunny climate, for which millions of people passionately yearn. Unlike the situation in Florida, surface water in the Southwest is usually not a problem (although drinking water often is). To make the area even more appealing, the region has an abundance of cheap land. Land promotion was spurred further when many big western ranches were broken up during the 1950s and 1960s as a result of rising taxes and land values.

"Southwest Land Rush: Promoters Push Sales Throughout the U.S.," headlined a *Wall Street Journal* dispatch from El Paso, Texas, in the summer of 1960. Reported the *Journal's* Neil Maxwell: "This dry, desert-like land 30 miles east of El Paso, devoid of life as far as the eye can see, is scheduled to become part of a metropolis which some 3 million people will call home — if promises of its promoters and dreams of thousands of $7.50-down, $5-a-month speculators pan out. Only the lack of population is impressive now . . . humans

are far outnumbered by coyotes, bobcats, and lesser animals."
At the time the *Journal* article was written, more than 60,000
lots in the area had been sold to buyers throughout the U.S.

El Paso's land rush was triggered by a 1959 announcement
of plans by the Horizon Corporation for Horizon City, a
"metropolis of the future" with a projected population of
1.5 million on a tract of 100 square miles. Horizon City was
quickly dwarfed in size when El Paso developer Harlan E.
O'Leary gave birth nearby to Sun City, covering no less than
130 square miles. O'Leary's younger brother, Gerald P. O'Leary,
came along with Wilco Addition, adjoining Horizon City on
the north and containing 30 square miles. When orders
started coming in for lots in those projects, more than a
half dozen other promoters arrived on the scene.

Neil Maxwell wrote: "Of the dozen or so 'suburbs' of
Horizon City, Wilco Addition is rare in that signs of actual
development are visible. Driving eight miles over a sandy
road from the highway, a visitor sees neat patterns of 'streets'
scraped into the prairie by a bulldozer and stretching across
the land until they reach hills. 'We've already cut 700 miles
of roads, and we're going to cut 700 miles more,' says Gilbert
Asher, one of several Mt. Franklin Homes vice-presidents.
'We started out with nearly 75,000 lots to sell, and we've already sold more than 41,000 of them,' he says."

By 1972, however, El Paso's stupendous population ex-
plosion had yet to materialize. Between 1960 and 1970 the
city added only 40,775 people, bringing the total to 317,462.

El Paso's land rush was merely a microcosm of a pattern
that had occurred throughout much of the region. Around
Albuquerque, Phoenix, Tucson, and numerous other communities promoters were grabbing up huge tracts of rural
land and selling hundreds of thousands of lots on the national
market. Already the selling tactics employed by many of the
subdividers were prompting expressions of deep concern on
the part of realty boards, Better Business Bureaus, and state
officials. "Some of them sell lots by mail to people who can't
see what they are buying, and they sell to Mexicans who

can't afford it but have always dreamed of owning a piece of land — any land," remarked Dennis Wagner, an El Paso realtor.

There was plenty of hoopla, some of it as outlandish as anything to come out of the first Florida land boom. One developer sent an airplane aloft to scatter currency in denominations up to $100 as a crowd raiser. Another staged an Easter egg hunt on his property. In Albuquerque a promoter buried silver dollars on lots for sale, invited parents to bring their "junior prospectors" to dig for them, and pitched the parents on lot purchases while the treasure hunt was in progress. Brochures and newspaper ads offered, among other things, "America's most exciting land bargain, adjacent to the world's most beautifully planned city," "planned profits," and a "golden opportunity to cash in on the explosive expansion now taking place in the booming Southwest."

Explosive expansion? Not quite. In May, 1962, the state of New Mexico tried to auction off 12,500 acres of choice suburban land just a mile and a half south of Albuquerque's city limits. Despite a national advertising campaign that produced inquiries from 500 prospective buyers, only about 20 bidders showed up; after 4 days of listless bidding only 8 out of the 272 available tracts were sold. The state had expected to receive $15 million to $18 million for the property; it got $398,999.

Even at its nonsensical zenith the first Florida land boom never produced a stunt quite like the one pulled off by Robert P. McCulloch, a Los Angeles real estate tycoon. In 1963 McCulloch began building a new and isolated community in the Arizona desert called Lake Havasu City. The development was programmed to house 75,000 people by 1980. When there was no stampede of people wanting to settle there (the 1971 population was about 7,500), McCulloch started looking for something — anything — to drum up more business. He found it astride the Thames River in London. The fabled London Bridge had fallen into disrepair and was for sale by the British government.

McCulloch bought it for $2,460,000 and had it dismantled

stone by stone. It was shipped to America and reassembled across a small manmade river in Lake Havasu City at a cost of $8 million. For $500,000 more he had two gigantic peppermint-striped medieval tents erected on the structure. The developer said that the span would attract 5 million tourists a year, that they would spend $80 million, and that some of them could be persuaded to buy property in the development. (The bridge's value as a promotional gimmick remains to be seen, but one can't help thinking about all the community facilities that could have been built with those millions. "Here we are with a bridge to nowhere, and the hospital isn't even built yet," snorted one irreverent resident.)

In October, 1971, the transplanted span was dedicated with ceremonies that would have awed George Merrick himself. On hand were 40,000 gawking spectators, dozens of celebrities, 30,000 balloons, 5,000 pigeons, the Lord Mayor of London, and a coterie of his retainers, dressed in seventeenth-century armor and red cloth.

What happened next was described by *Newsweek* magazine:

> At the electric moment when the Lord Mayor snipped a red ribbon to open the bridge, bedlam erupted on the tranquil desert. The white pigeons (rented at $2 apiece) raced skyward together with the rainbow-colored balloons. A five-story-high helium-filled bag adorned with the red, white, and blue of the Union Jack soared aloft, passing some 30 descending skydivers in multicolored parachutes who trailed purple smoke from canisters attached to their legs. Then a blast of trumpets heralded a seemingly endless parade of bands, girls, horses, and floats.

One of McCulloch's British guests gasped: "It's all quite mad. It could only happen in America."

By 1962 the operations of the less scrupulous concerns were attracting a good deal of attention. Multicolored ads for an Oregon development, for instance, showed cattle grazing contentedly in green meadows, seemingly a wonderful place for a retired couple to buy five acres for $900, with payments of $17 a month. But state officials found that the soil at the site would support little more than sagebrush and jack-rabbits.

A tract of 3.5 million acres in Brazil was described in the brochures of American promoters as a sure-fire investment at $10 an acre because the property was in an "ideal" location for homesteading and was bound to appreciate in value. In reality the land was "for the most part in an impenetrable jungle infested by swarms of insects," postal inspectors learned from U.S. foreign service officers. They ordered sales halted.

There were literally thousands of equally fraudulent promotions. In 1962 the National Better Business Bureau, Inc., now the Council of Better Business Bureaus, Inc., warned that the "biggest land scandal in American history" was developing in Florida and the Southwest. Nathaniel Kossack, chief of the fraud section of the U.S. Department of Justice, termed land fraud "one of the most active confidence games" in existence.

J. Fred Talley, Arizona's real estate commissioner, declared: "Our present pie-in-the-sky land schemers make the promoters who sold underwater land in Florida, pawned off worthless stock to unsuspecting widows, and promoted gold mines that didn't exist look like amateurs relegated to the bush leagues."

Such statements didn't go unnoticed by the national press. A number of mass-circulation publications carried detailed accounts of what was happening in land sales, including *Reader's Digest, Newsday, Life, Wall Street Journal,* and *Saturday Evening Post,* which led off a major article in 1963 with this observation:

> One of the ugliest swindles being run in America today is the mail-order sale of worthless land. Across the country last year thousands of Americans, dreaming of a place in the sun, fell victim to unscrupulous promoters peddling grossly misrepresented homesites in Utah, Arizona, New Mexico, Oregon, Nevada, Florida — and even Panama, Costa Rica and Brazil.

A flurry of mail fraud prosecutions followed public exposure, but penalties were usually light. For example, the

most celebrated swindle of that era was Lake Mead Rancheros
in Arizona, in which desolate cactus country was advertised
as "Livable Now!" (See Chapter 6.) The three principal of-
fenders drew fines of $10,000, $7,500, and $5,000, respectively,
plus suspended prison sentences; they had taken in an estimated $1.8 million.

Robert N. Golubin, a former Los Angeles taxi driver with
a voluminous police record, drew three years' imprisonment
for fraud in the sale of some 35,000 lots in three Taos County,
New Mexico, subdivisions named Tres Piedras Estates, Carson
Estates, and Ranchos de Taos Estates. Golubin's Great Southwestern Land Company sold "chances" on lots at fairs around
the country. Almost everyone who had taken a "chance" was
subsequently notified that he or she was a "winner" and
could claim the "prize" — a lot — by paying $49.30 or $52.50
in "closing costs." Salesmen then tried to sell "winners" more
lots by issuing glowing descriptions of the surrounding
scenery and claiming that water, roads, and utilities were
readily accessible. Actually the property was composed almost
entirely of volcanic rock, roads were impassable for four
months a year due to heavy snow, and water was practically
unobtainable. Golubin and his confederates extracted $3.5
million from victims before the law stepped in.

In 1964 11 men were indicted on mail fraud charges in
connection with a Nevada-Utah promotion called Gamble
Ranch. The indictment charged, among other things, that
the defendants advertised that the 930-square-mile ranch consisted of "lush farm land" with "many springs," and that
"electricity and power are in, ready to be used today — not
tomorrow." In truth the soil there is alkaline and thus detri-
mental to many farming operations; to obtain water it would
be necessary to drill wells costing several times the purchase
price of the land parcels; and existing power facilities were
sufficient only for about 75 more connections. California
contractor Douglas McCann, one tract buyer who took the
trouble to visit the property, exclaimed later:

"I was dumbfounded. The city they talked about was just

a deserted railroad siding. And to go fishing on the lake we went over a road filled with the damnedest boulders you have ever seen. The lake looked more like a hog wallow, a spawning place for mosquitoes."

In 1966 three men accused of using misleading advertising to sell land in eastern Oregon were fined $4,500 each and placed on one year's probation. They were Richard D. Walker, of Los Angeles, John M. Phillips, Jr., of Evanston, Illinois, and Jack Cecil Cherbo, all officers of the Harney County Land Development Corporation. They had entered a plea of no contest to the charges.

The authorities also closed in on Gerald P. O'Leary. He was convicted of fraud in El Paso, put on probation for five years, and fined $5,000. Prosecutors estimated that he fleeced the public of at least $60,000.

These and other prosecutions, together with the attendant notoriety, dealt a severe blow to the land sales business. Sales and earnings dropped precipitously, even those of companies regarded as reputable. Some outfits folded their tents, and others revised their selling techniques, adopting a more subtle approach. Florida companies suffered an added setback from the Cuban missile crisis of 1962; the thought of a Russian rocket arsenal 90 miles from Miami soured many people on the idea of owning Florida land.

These misfortunes were followed by the adoption of stiffer land sales regulations in some states and the enactment of truth-in-land-sales laws. Even so, by 1967 most of the leading land companies were doing as well or better than before. Their talent for selling and showmanship seemed keener than ever.

4

Subdividing the Universe

*Of all man's activities, his use of the land has
the most far-reaching impact on the environment.*
— Rogers C. B. Morton,
U.S. Secretary of the Interior

THE most expeditious way to make big money
in real estate is to acquire a large tract of raw land, cut it
up into smaller parcels, and sell the parcels at a profit, with
or without such improvements as streets and sanitation facilities. Most of the vast fortunes amassed from land speculation
were produced in this way.

Land in the United States has traditionally been subdivided on a speculative basis in advance of market demand.
In other words, developers usually stake out building lots
or erect housing before they have purchase or rental com-
mitments. The developers are confident that, because of population growth or human mobility, occupants will soon appear
— and usually they do.

This system generally works well when the creation of
subdivisions is controlled by intelligent planning or zoning
laws or by legitimate demand for living space. Responsible
home builders, community developers, and architects of quality

58

"new towns" seldom develop more building lots than necessary to meet immediate or anticipated housing needs. They also limit the size of their developments in order to keep them compact and efficient.

An outstanding example of meticulous community planning is Columbia, Maryland, an award-winning new city in the making, on 14 thousand acres of lush, rolling countryside in the rapidly growing corridor between Baltimore and Washington, D.C. When it has been completed, in 1980, Columbia will provide housing for 110,000 people and employment for 30,000. It will have 70 schools, 50 churches, several parks, a full range of cultural and recreational activities, handy suburban and downtown shopping facilities, 3,000 acres of forests, 26 miles of riding trails, 5 lakes, and 3 scenic stream valleys. Five square miles have been set aside as permanent open space.

Started in 1964, Columbia is a product of gutsy enterprise, imagination, planning expertise, exhaustive research, and huge infusions of risk capital from such financial giants as the Connecticut General Life Insurance Company, the Chase Manhattan Bank, the Teachers Insurance & Annuity Association, Morgan Guaranty Trust Company, Equitable Life Assurance Society, John Hancock Mutual Life Insurance Company, and others. Already more than $300 million have been spent on land, improvements, and construction.

"Our first objective was to build a real city, to provide what we would call a balanced city, a comprehensive city," asserts the developer of Columbia, James Rouse, president of the Rouse Company of Baltimore. "We would be accounting as fully as we could for all the things that people do in a city of 110,000."

Before the first earth was turned, the company spent months preparing economic and population analyses and ascertaining what a city of 110,000 would need in the way of jobs, schools, churches, hospitals, stores, restaurants, hotels, and the manifold other requisites of a self-contained model city. In working up their master blueprint Columbia's planners drew maps showing every landmark, grove of trees, hill, valley, road, and stream and then laid out patterns of development that would take the most advantage of these features and preserve the beauty of the landscape.

Columbia opened in June, 1967. During its first five years it attracted some 600 industries, 300 businesses, and more than 20,000 residents.

Money, inspiration, know-how, boldness, drive, and conscientiousness are essential for putting a top-flight planned community on the map. Columbia and Reston, Virginia, a 7,400-acre development 18 miles southwest of Washington, D.C., are the two most widely admired of the 50 or so large planned communities that have appeared in the United States since World War II. Those two are in the vanguard of a growing movement to create scores, possibly hundreds, of "new towns" around the country in order to alleviate excruciating population pressures on existing cities, to avoid the evils of urban sprawl, and to improve the quality of living for millions of people. They are not cheap.

Acquiring land, making improvements, and completing the initial construction may require more than $50 million in "front money." For qualified developers, however, such undertakings are no longer quite so formidable as they once were. Congress, finally recognizing a need to encourage quality development, provided for federal assistance through the Housing and Urban Development (HUD) Acts of 1968 and 1970. By 1972 some $136 million in loan guarantees had been committed to seven new town projects: Riverton, New York; Jonathan, Minnesota; Park Forest South, Illinois; St. Charles, Maryland; Maumelle, Arkansas; Flower Mound, Texas; and Cedar-Riverside, a "new town in town" in the center of Minneapolis, Minnesota.

To receive HUD aid a project must meet stiff eligibility requirements. Briefly, it must provide a substantial number of low-cost housing units and equal opportunities in housing and employment for minority groups. Open spaces must be provided in generous amounts. Above all, a development must be balanced, providing for industry as well as housing and recreation facilities. Both Columbia and Reston place great emphasis on attracting local job opportunities for residents. Columbia has enticed no fewer than 44 companies to its industrial park, including a $250-million General Electric plant with an employment capacity of 12,000 people.

With U.S. population continuing to swell — although not nearly at the rate that the land hustlers would have us believe — the National Committee on Urban Growth Policy has recommended the creation, by the end of this century, of 100 new communities of at least 100,000 population, plus 10 new cities of 1 million or more. Even if this should be done, the bulk of any population increase would still have to be absorbed by existing metropolitan centers, which are already wracked by overcrowding, crime, pollution, congestion, and financial shortages.

So much for positive planning. The sad fact is that despite the critical need for better places in which to live, American land use policies and regulations often encourage the worst possible development practices. The builders of Columbia and Reston might have made more money with far less effort had they elected simply to sell lots without concerning themselves with what resulted. Selling lots can be vastly more profitable than community building, and it requires much less capital.

The antithesis of Columbia, Reston and such like achievements are what are called "premature subdivisions" or "fast-buck subdivisions." These are developments — "promotions" is perhaps a better word for describing most of them — in which the primary objective is the selling of great numbers of lots, usually with a minimum of improvements.

Premature subdivisions can be found almost everywhere. The market for real estate of dubious value seems to be limitless. In any representative group of human beings there will be individuals who are stupid, gullible,* unfamiliar

---

*Some people's lack of comprehension is astounding. In 1970 and 1971 the federal Office of Interstate Land Sales Registration (OILSR) sponsored televised warnings about land swindles, using "Rainbow City" as an example of

with land economics, impressionable, or vulnerable to flattery or high pressure. Misconceptions about land and land investing are commonplace. As Sylvan Kamm, a consultant with the Urban Land Institute (ULI), a research and information organization, has noted in the ULI publication *Urban Land,* Americans have greatly exaggerated notions about what land is worth — notions that have contributed to "grossly disproportionate" increases in land prices. Land has a powerful, almost hypnotic appeal for millions of people, and the desire to possess it is deep seated.

For these reasons glib promoters are able to sell — usually at ridiculous prices — fantastic numbers of "homesites" or acreage tracts that may not be habitable for generations, if ever.

Nobody knows how many unneeded, remote, barely accessible, poorly planned, or uninhabitable subdivisions have been platted and sold in the United States. The problem has gotten little attention, partly because relatively few people know that it exists and partly because, until recently, it has not been particularly troublesome except in scattered areas. Today, however, premature subdivisions are being created on an unprecedented scale, and the situation is taking on increasingly disquieting dimensions — not only because so many people are being rooked but also because so much land is being wastefully exploited, often with serious and irreversible damage to the environment.

"Land use . . . is the key to all the rest of our environmental problems," the *Washington Post* observed in a 1971 editorial. "The nature of one development — whether it is a country club or a chemical plant — determines the nature of everything around it; it affects the quality of the air and the water and the lives of perhaps thousands of people. And yet as a nation we still subscribe to the old 'pioneer land ethic,'

---

a typical phony offering. Before long the agency was getting letters from people asking how they could get information about buying lots in Rainbow City. (The OILSR also received a blistering letter from the mayor of Rainbow City, Alabama, a hamlet that somehow escaped the notice of OILSR researchers, who had picked what they thought was a fictitious name.)

which holds that the owner of the land has the God-given right to do with it as he damned pleases."

Roots of the pioneer land ethic run deep. Land speculation is as indigenous to the United States as is mass production. The premature subdivision is older than the republic. During and after the colonial period enterprising land hustlers engaged in what was called "land jobbing," or "town jobbing," a type of speculation that was strikingly similar to many of today's promotional offerings. When new areas were opened for settlement, land jobbers moved in, bought up large tracts of acreage that looked promising as town sites, and sold off parcels. Some cities actually were started this way — Baltimore, Maryland, Detroit, Michigan, Dayton and Cincinnati, Ohio, for examples — but for every town jobbing venture that succeeded as many as 100 collapsed. A description of how town jobbing usually turned out was recorded by John Biggs, an Englishman who took a keen interest in the subject:

> A speculator makes out a plan of a city with its streets, squares, and avenues, quays and wharves, public buildings and monuments. The streets are lotted, the houses numbered, and the squares called after Franklin or Washington. The city itself has some fine names, perhaps Troy or Antioch. This is engraved and forthwith advertised and hung up in as many steamboats and hotels as the speculator's interest may command. All this time the city is a mere vision. Its very site is on the fork of some river in the Far West, 500 miles beyond civilization, probably underwater or surrounded by dense forests and impassable swamps. Emigrants have been repeatedly defrauded out of their money by transactions so extremely gross as hardly to be credited.

A floodtide of such speculation engulfed the Midwest and the Northwest during the 1830s and afterward. "The platting, marketing, buying, and selling of nonexistent future cities . . . was an enterprise that captured the attention, imagination, and capital of all those within reach," Malcolm J. Rohrbough wrote in *The Land Office Business*. "Rivals vied with one

another in extolling the virtues of their Athenses, and everyone found buyers."

One of the more flamboyant promotions of the last century
was New Babylon, situated on the Missouri River in eastern
Kansas. Widely advertised, New Babylon was hailed by its
creators as a future industrial and transportation center in
the path of western migration, destined to become another
Chicago or St. Louis. In his book, *Beyond the Mississippi*,
Albert D. Richardson commented: "If the newcomer had the
unusual wisdom to visit the prophetic city before purchasing
lots, he would in most cases find one or two rough cabins,
with perhaps a tent and an Indian canoe in the river." Today
the area is flat farmland.

Town site speculations dwindled with the passing of the
frontier, but excessive subdividing continued in many places.
A federal government report published in 1940 noted: "The
fever of land speculation, of trying to sell at an artificially
high price land that might at some remote future time have
genuine value from the outward thrust of population, has
permeated the fiber of every portion of the country. Few have
paused to estimate the rate of possible future growth. It was
assured by the land peddler and his gullible purchasers that
population increase was inevitable, that the quick way to
riches was to buy land and await the onward march of development, to sell at a high price and buy again."

The report cited a few "random illustrations." On Long
Island, it said, "enough lots are staked off to make suburban-
ites of the inhabitants of the five boroughs of New York."
In 1926 around the town of Islip there were 20,000 lots for
which owners had stopped paying taxes, yet 9,000 new lots
were platted during one 18-month period. "As a result, the
real estate market was trying to move about four times as
many lots as there were then families in the town," declared
the report. Then some 50 estates in the same area were sold
for future subdividing. By July, 1926, 40,587 out of 86,349
lots had reverted to the ownership of the county because
taxes had not been paid, but subdividers continued to plat
still more.

Of 375,000 lots in Cleveland in 1929, 175,000 were vacant, the report goes on to say. Chicago was said to have had enough platted suburban land in the mid 1930s to house 18 million people. Seventy-five percent of the total platted area of Burbank, California, and 53 percent of the platted land in Los Angeles County was vacant at the time the report was drafted. Fifty percent of the land in Portland, Maine, was empty, and 66 percent of the lot area of Duluth, Minnesota, likewise was unoccupied, as was 30 percent of the lot area of El Paso, Texas. Outside St. Louis there were more than 100,000 vacant lots.

It has been estimated that the total acreage subdivided in Florida during the 1920s land boom was sufficient to house the population of the entire United States at that time. Nobody knows exactly how much Florida land has been sold off in small chunks by promoters because so many subdivisions are unplatted, but the amount must be astronomical. A single company, the General Development Corporation, has platted more that 200,000 acres (312 square miles), enough land for six cities the size of Boston (1970 population: 628,215). General Development, moreover, is only one of hundreds of Florida subdividers, though it is true that as of 1972 a total of only about 30,000 persons were living in its seven communities.

Perhaps the most dramatic evidence of indiscriminate subdividing can be found in records that show how many lots stand vacant and unused around the country. As part of the Census of Governments the U.S. Bureau of the Census uses tax rolls to compile totals of occupied and unoccupied lots in each state every five years. In reporting the totals the bureau also provides a breakdown showing what percentage of all locally assessed urban property is vacant.

The most recent lot census was taken in 1966. Figures for selected states, together with comparable figures compiled for 1961, are shown in Table 1. It will be noted that warm-climate states, in which land promoters are especially active, have by far the highest proportion of empty lots. Florida, the population of which totaled 6,671,162 in 1970, counted

1,004,000 idle lots, while New York state, with 17,979,712
people, had 626,000. Arizona, with 1,752,122 citizens, reported
233,000 vacant lots. The total number of vacant lots for the
United States in 1966 was 14,250,000, enough to provide homes
for as many as 57 million people.

TABLE 1
Numbers of Vacant Lots in the United States and
Selected States*

	1966		1961		1970
	Number of vacant lots	Percent of total lots	Number of vacant lots	Percent of total lots	Population
U.S.	14,250,000	19.0	12,876,000	19.1	200,251,326
Ariz.	233,000	36.2	153,000	29.5	1,752,122
Calif.	1,009,000	16.9	1,010,000	18.4	19,715,490
Colo.	141,000	18.1	100,000	13.3	2,178,176
Fla.	1,004,000	34.5	751,000	33.4	6,671,162
N. Mex.	118,000	31.3	70,000	20.3	998,287
N.Y.	626,000	15.4	681,000	17.6	17,979,712
Nev.	50,000	27.6	17,000	16.3	481,893
Ohio	996,000	25.3	1,016,000	26.3	10,542,030
Oreg.	142,000	17.0	121,000	16.2	2,056,171
Pa.	527,000	13.8	457,000	12.3	11,669,565
Tex.	1,515,000	17.0	936,000	19.4	10,989,123
Utah	64,000	16.8	50,000	13.5	1,060,631
Wyo.	10,000	8.9	15,000	12.9	328,591

Bear in mind that even though these data were obtained
before the great upsurge in second-home developments, the
rate of increase in vacant lots was greater than the rate of
increase in people. The U.S. population rose less than 6
percent between 1961 and 1966; the number of vacant lots
climbed almost 10 percent. The differential was even greater
in some individual states. In Florida, for example, vacant

---

* Source: U.S. Department of Commerce, Bureau of the Census, Census of
Governments, 1967.

lots multiplied by about 25 percent, while the population swelled by less than 14 percent.

A committee that investigated land-selling abuses in Florida in the early 1960s reported that "certain features have always been present" in land boom cycles. "Land speculators get large tracts, often on credit," the panel said. "These tracts are subdivided and sold in small parcels. Scattered building takes place, making a need for public services and the consequent increase in taxes and assessments. Vacant land, generally purchased by small-income families, becomes tax delinquent. Tax arrearages and penalty assessments exceed the value of lots. Clearing title is costly and slow, and owners are hard to locate, so small parcels have stayed 'dead' and usused. Original improvements are inadequate."

In Florida and elsewhere premature subdividing has inflated land prices artificially by diminishing the supply; caused patchy, or "leapfrogging,"* development patterns, which raise costs of governmental services; produced rural slums; clouded land titles; and removed from tax rolls large areas of land with income-producing potential, thus increasing the tax load for other property owners. Prices of single-family dwellings have soared beyond the reach of millions of American families. The biggest contributor to the skyrocketing cost of housing is the price of land. In the decade that ended in 1966 average costs of sites for homes financed by the Federal Housing Administration rose from 14.2 percent to 18.2 percent of the total cost. To be sure, premature subdividing is just one of several reasons for this escalation, but it is a significant factor in many places.

"In the course of transforming land from rural to urban use, enormous values are created, which encourage speculative activities that reinforce the tendency toward higher prices,"

---

* The term "leapfrogging" refers to subdivisions that must be located farther and farther from the center of population because of the unavailability of suitable land closer in. The greater the distance from the city, the greater the traveling time for commuters and the higher the cost, in many cases, of access roads, utility lines, and services such as refuse collection.

the National Commission on Urban Problems reported in a 1968 study entitled *U.S. Land Prices — Directions and Dynamics.* "Higher prices, in turn, have an adverse effect on the possibility of producing low-cost housing, and the speculative holdings may create inefficient and otherwise undesirable land-use patterns," the commission continued. According to reliable estimates, at least 31 million new housing units will be needed by 1978, but the already slim chances of obtaining that staggering total are made slimmer yet by destructive use of the land.

"Vast amounts of valuable land beclouded by premature subdivision remain wasted," said the October, 1971, issue of *Appraisal Journal,* a quarterly publication of the American Institute of Real Estate Appraisers. "At the same time the need for housing and other sites is leading to tremendously expensive proposals for site acquisition." The article was written by two professional planners, Stephen Sussna and Jack Kirchhoff, who reported: "Premature subdivision has frustrated proper land development and investment potential in numerous strategic locations across the United States." Declaring that a "thorough examination [of the problem] on a national scale is crucial," the authors asserted that "premature subdivision represents an important problem which is both *widespread* and which involves large amounts of potentially *valuable* land." Moreover, because so many promotional lots are sold to low- or modest-income individuals, any construction that does result is likely to be inferior. "Often, rural slums occupying *valuable* locations have been the end product," Sussna and Kirchhoff observed.

A similar point was made by several witnesses who testified at U.S. Senate land-fraud hearings during the 1960s. W. Dan Bell, president of the Denver Better Business Bureau, had this to say:

> As a result of depredation of land use by many . . . promotions, titles of hundreds of thousands of acres have been placed in jeopardy [in Colorado]. In the areas where no actual physical

development occurred, the various claims to title by many persons in various states who hold contracts or have paid money for specified lots, much of which is not yet of record, will cloud the properties for years to come, and will deter future development. In those areas, partially developed but abandoned by the developers, shacks, huts, and deterioration of property discourage proper development. And county governments are faced with mounting costs involved in growing tax delinquencies that occur.

Despite investigations, subdividers seem to be more active than ever in Colorado. The Rocky Mountain Center on Environment estimated in 1972 that bulldozers were preparing no less than 1 million acres for development. "Own a piece of Colorado!" cry the developers, and buyers appear from nowhere.

In their *Appraisal Journal* article Sussna and Kirchhoff maintain that the "necessity for assembling large land tracts near our large cities is intensifying, and despite the obvious evils of premature subdivisions, they still continue." That's putting the situation mildly. The explosive growth of interstate land selling has added new and even more alarming dimensions to the problem.

The indiscriminate subdividing that occurred prior to the 1950s was, for the most part, the work of relatively small local promoters. When multimillion-dollar corporations with international sales networks began moving into land development in a big way, the rate at which raw land was converted into lots and small acreage tracts took a sudden turn upward. During one 18-month period in the early 1960s, for example, 630 separate subdivisions were platted on the cactus-covered deserts of Mohave County, Arizona, a county almost twice the size of Massachusetts but which counted a population of only 25,110 in 1970. The territory that has been subdivided in the vicinity of Albuquerque, New Mexico (population 242,411), could accommodate four cities the size of Baltimore, Maryland (population 895,222). Other such examples abound.

Many of the offerings of present-day land companies are, in varying degrees, premature subdivisions. As was noted in Chapter 1, installment land companies make most of their money from the sale of lots. A number of outfits do no building at all, and with others construction is secondary. A land company will usually buy several hundred acres of raw land, normally in a sparsely settled area, and will sign options that give the company the right to buy several thousand additional acres. Next the company builds a small core community — a few model homes, perhaps a golf course or a clubhouse, even a recreation center. At the same time large numbers of lots in the development are put on the national market. If sales go well, money starts coming in from down payments and monthly payments on lot-purchase contracts, generating a cash flow. Part of the cash-flow money is used to enlarge the developed area. Then options are exercised, more lots are staked out and put on the market, and the cash flow increases. Thus lot buyers provide the life blood of the development, actually helping to *finance* it. They, not the land company, supply most of the front money, and lot buyers assume most of the risks, which often are substantial.* If the cash flow diminishes, development usually stops unless the developer can somehow raise more cash from other sources or unless he has posted surety bonds to guarantee the completion of promised improvements. Usually such bonds are *not* put up.

Indeed, an installment land company that is publicly owned, as many are, is a real money machine. Its initial working capital comes from stock buyers, and much of its operating money comes from lot buyers. Yet all a lot buyer gets in return for risking his money, as a rule, is a contract in which the developer agrees to convey an improved homesite to the purchaser several years in the future. The contract probably specifies further that the purchaser can lose his equity if he

---

*With a large percentage of lot selling ventures, the risks are so high that banks, insurance companies, and other major lenders refuse to finance them.

misses two or three payments. Such contracts, unlike stocks, bonds, or mutual-fund shares, are seldom readily salable. Even when a development grows and prospers, the lot buyer may lose money, for reasons that will be discussed in Chapter 6.

Thus the method used by installment land companies to develop communities is the opposite of that used by the creators of Columbia, Reston, and other major planned communities, who amass considerable amounts of front money before they break ground. (At Columbia less than 10 percent of the lots are sold to individuals; nearly all of the building sites are conveyed to home builders and commercial developers.) This is not to say that the lot-selling approach, while frowned on by a number of land-use authorities, such as the Urban Land Institute, is not legitimate; if competently administered, it is capable of producing good communities. But there are fundamental weaknesses in the system, which often work to the detriment of both lot buyers and the general public. Because a project's success is dependent on lot sales rather than housing demand, the pressure to sell lots is enormous — giving rise to questionable sales practices — and if a project fails, the area in which it is located may inherit an ugly ghost town and lose tax revenue because of abandoned properties.

Moreover, the communities that result from installment land selling often have characteristics regarded by some as undesirable. The communities are usually located in remote areas, where land is cheap. In most cases there is little, if any, industry nearby and consequently few jobs. Urban features such as culture centers, airports, hospitals, department stores, and government service offices are apt to be miles away. Because so many lots are bought as speculative investments by people who have no intention of living on them, huge patches of the development may remain vacant for generations. A lot owner who does build may find himself a half mile from his nearest neighbor.

The heavy emphasis on lot selling can be inherently self-defeating in some instances. The GAC Corporation, for example, has promised to install a water system at Rio Rico, its 55,000-acre offering in Arizona. But, says Hoyt C. Duty, senior legal counsel for the California Department of Real Estate, "The state won't permit them to put in utilities unless there's a demand sufficient to provide a return that would justify the expense. We find that in this subdivision and others similar to it, from 97 to 99 percent of the lots are sold for investment. The buyers do not intend to go there and live. So how can there be any demand for utilities? It's like a dog chasing his tail."

For such reasons as this California bars out-of-state subdivision offerings in which buyers must wait for more than four years for improvements, and such improvements must be guaranteed by performance bonds or other financial security. (See Chapter 11.)

The land companies argue that their approach is no different from that of a corporation that sells shares of stock to raise capital for financing a business venture or an unproved idea. But it is *very* different. If a business goes bankrupt, the only ones hurt, as a rule, are the owners, stockholders, and creditors. On the other hand, if a subdivision flops and lots are abandoned, the county or state loses tax revenue, and the loss must be made up by other taxpayers. If enough subdivided land becomes idle, the aforementioned effects on land values, development patterns, and housing may occur.

When local governments provide services to new subdivisions — street maintenance, schools, fire and police protection, refuse collection, and the like — the cost often is higher than the increase in revenue from property taxes. This can be a numbing blow to taxpayers in surrounding areas. Maryland State Senator William J. Goodman charges that excessive development is causing the state to go bankrupt. In an attempt to turn back the tide he has introduced legislation that would empower the state to declare how much land could be subdivided. "I look at master plans throughout the state with absolute grief," he asserts. "Daily, the loss of our prime agricultural land, forests, and coastal areas goes unabated with local government failing to examine the requirements for new governmental facilities and services dictated by the feverish pace of new construction."

After a year's research Goodman discovered that while his own county taxes soared 500 percent between 1953 and 1970, tax revenue rose only 120 percent in the same period. "This is the price that older residents of Prince George's County paid for development in addition to flooding, sewer problems, and air pollution," he adds.

The term "new town" is being used with increasing regularity by land companies, although few, if any, of their projects can qualify for the title. At this writing, no installment land company is participating in the federal assistance program to encourage new town construction. New towns do not lend themselves to precise definitions, but the genuine ones are self-contained, self-sufficient communities, in which employment is available and the developers are more concerned with building than with selling lots. One of the newest land company projects to be billed as a "new town" is Poinciana, an offering of GAC Properties, Inc. Located 30 miles south of Orlando, Florida, and 60 miles east of Tampa, Poinciana is spread over 47,300 acres (compared with Columbia's 14,000 acres) and has a population capacity of 250,000. In advertising supplements that appeared in 20 metropolitan newspapers in early 1972, the development was hailed as "A 'new town' designed from scratch, to avoid the problems of most towns. . . . It's surrounded by fresh water lakes and laced through with ancient forests of moss-hung oak and cypress. A place where deer and quail will be your neighbors, because we're inviting them to stay." (Actually, Florida authorities have ordained that 18,430 of the 47,300 acres must be preserved as open space to minimize the risks of pollution.) Poinciana may indeed become a bustling semitropical El Dorado, but lot buyers will be supplying most of the funds.

In their eagerness to sell lots, land companies frequently produce subdivisions that are grotesque in shape or pre-

posterous in size. Silver Spring Shores, a 17,300-acre (27 square
mile) offering of the AMREP Corporation outside Ocala,
Florida, is 20 miles long and about 2 miles wide; on a map it
looks like an underfed boa constrictor. Port Charlotte, the
flagship community of Florida's General Development Corporation, occupies 100,000 acres (153 square miles), more
than twice the territory of the nation's capital. Between 1956
and 1972 General Development sold over 90,000 lots in Port
Charlotte, but only 22,500 persons settled there.

The ITT Community Development Corporation's Palm
Coast, located in a region of truck farms and palmetto
patches between St. Augustine and Daytona Beach, Florida,
is 30 miles long and spread over more land area than Philadelphia (population 1,926,529). Around the isolated little
(population 8,343) town of Deming, New Mexico, Select
Western Lands, Inc., a company headed by former New Mexico
State Representative Carter W. Kirk, has subdivided some 54
square miles into half-acre "ranchettes" — in an area larger than
Minneapolis (population 431,977). Unlike Minneapolis, however, Deming Ranchettes are not situated on one contiguous
piece of real estate; the area consists of no fewer than 112
separate parcels scattered all around Deming. Some of the
parcels are 35 miles from the town.

"*Live Longer and Better in New Mexico*," trumpet ads
for Carter Kirk's offering. "Many sales are made to people
planning to retire here in the future," says Luna County
Clerk Ruth A. King. Yet the record of home construction
at Deming Ranchettes suggests that there are not very many
senior citizens who are willing to flee from civilization, set
up housekeeping on a windswept prairie 10 miles from the
nearest neighbor and 25 miles from the nearest settlement,
and live it up in their twilight years watching jackrabbits
and tumbleweed. Only 110 homes had been built on the
ranchettes as of 1971, although the properties went on the
national market in 1960.

No doubt, many, if not most, of the people who buy
ranchettes are swayed by advertised statements that allude

to "the inevitable rise in land values" and expect to make money on resales, and nobody can deny that values have gone up. The price of a homesite at Deming Ranchettes has jumped all the way from $199 to $299 in 10 years. The claim that Deming is "in the fastest-growing region in America" may be stretching facts a little, though. The town's population has climbed from 5,672 in 1950 to 8,343 in 1970, 2,660 new people in 20 years, or about 133 a year.

If tens of thousands of lot ,buyers ever do descend on Luna County, pure chaos could result. Hospitals, bus lines, government services, and other public facilities could be overwhelmed by the influx. "People moving from the East to this area expect the services they received when they paid much higher taxes, and, of course, this area is not developed that extensively," notes Mrs. King. "Because of the scattered development there are no central water facilities. . . .I certainly recommend that people buying property here come and look it over before they buy and get facts and figures about well drilling, utilities, etc."

One of the most horrific examples of profligate subdividing is California City, 110 miles northeast of Los Angeles on the windswept, semiarid Mojave Desert. In a place where farmers had gone broke in 18 months because of high winds and blowing sand, a group headed by developer N. K. Mendelsohn bought up 100,000 acres (153 square miles) for $109 an acre, staked off 90,000 lots, announced the inception of a "planned city," and began selling the lots for $9,000 each. By 1969 some 32,000 parcels had been sold to people throughout the United States and in Germany and the Philippines, for a total of $102 million. The population in 1969 totaled 869, and while Mendelsohn* attempted to attract industry — and did provide some recreation and

---

* California City was acquired in 1969 by Great Western United, a conglomerate with milling, sugar, and pizza franchise interests. Mendelsohn was ousted. William White, Jr., Great Western United's president, said he was attracted to land development in part by the "incredible" profit margins that can be realized.

community facilities (using over $6 million in public financing) — there is no significant industrial development there, and the inhabitants are almost entirely dependent on the developers for employment.

Although it is California's third largest city in land area, California City lacks such essentials as a medical center or public transportation. In 1970 the Ralph Nader team that exposed California's land use practices uncovered a 100-page report on the development drafted by the California attorney-general's office. It said, in part:

> To prospective land buyers, California City is represented as a safe, secure real estate investment in a city with "abundant water." These representations are false. Purchasers desiring to sell find no ready market of buyers. Instead, when they are fortunate enough to resell they usually take a loss. . . .But this is no ordinary real estate sales scheme — Mendelsohn isn't trying to sell "land" and the public isn't really buying the "land." They are engaged in a grand illusion of creating wealth. . . . Mendelsohn has perfected the art of turning desert dust into gold — but only for himself.

Wildcat subdividing may ultimately inflict its worst damage on natural resources and the environment. "Steadily rising land prices have proved almost as much of a threat to the environment as pesticides or pollution," stated a *New York Times* editorial in 1968. "Farms which once served as natural 'green belts' between communities have given way to suburban sprawl as landowners reap larger profits from capital gains than from tilling the soil. Seashores and lake fronts are vulgarized and their natural defenses against erosion weakened as the developers rush to put up their jerry-built cottages."

Indeed, the environmental peril has loomed ever larger with the proliferation throughout the country of vacation or second-home developments, many of which feature lakes created by dammed streams, with others carved from forest land, mountain slopes, and lake shores. "The urban sprawl which has occurred to date only around urban centers will soon be seen in areas now remote," predicts Stephen C. Kaye, a New York City attorney who specializes in real estate law. In a statement supporting a tough federal land use policy Kaye told the U.S. Senate Committee on Interior and Insular Affairs in 1971:

> The proposed developments of land companies for sites scattered in present wilderness or agricultural areas make it a matter of grave national concern to bring all presently underdeveloped land under a form of rational, planned, land-use regulation. There are at least a dozen major U.S. corporations and many small ones which have acquired vast tracts of land, sometimes over 30,000 acres [46 square miles] for recreational, new town or commercial exploitation. The concern of these companies is not the environment, but profits. They will be motivated to exploit their investments with the profit motive foremost; the land is the raw material; nature the victim. The countryside can be expected to receive the same sympathetic treatment as the buffalo herds. These companies have the financial and physical power to lay waste vast tracts in about the same time as it took to devastate the buffalos.

Testifying before the same committee, Robert Knecht, mayor of Boulder, Colorado, and chairman of the National Cities Committee on Environment, asserted:

> There are just too many examples of what can be characterized as "The Rape of the Landscape" to counter any arguments that nothing needs to be done.
> Examples of harmful land-use activity abound. All across the nation, from the eastern shore of Maryland to the green mountains of Vermont, to the Arizona desert and the Sierra Nevada Mountains, we are witnessing the rapid spread of the so-called half-acre lot syndrome, pushed by land speculators to the point of turning some of our most beautiful recreational areas into second-home suburbias.

This type of development constitutes "the number one environmental problem in California," declares state sanitation engineer Glen Browning, who supervises public health water and sewer inspection in the northern and

central parts of California. "Speculative subdivisions ir-
reversibly change land-use patterns, and in some counties,
subdivisions have already outstripped water supplies."

Observes Harold Berliner, district attorney for Nevada
County: "Rural California is being carved up and committed
to completely unneeded urban development for the short-
term gain of a greedy handful of corporate subdividers."

By 1971 subdivisions covered 78 square miles of Nevada
County (population 26,500); it was estimated that if development continued at the rate in progress at that time, every
square foot of privately held land would be converted into
suburban-style lots by 1975. Erosion, pollution, and siltation
of streams already are serious problems in the county. The
waters of five major reservoirs have been adulterated by
development runoffs.

The Nader report on California land use warned:

> California's wild areas are in serious danger. Forests are
> leveled, the desert is bulldozed, lots are staked out and sold
> purely as speculative investments for alleged "second home"
> developments. Yet few houses are ever constructed. Those
> few lot buyers who do build homes face high costs and poor
> services.
>
> These development projects serve no housing or any other
> need. According to our data, there are now enough bulldozed,
> empty lots in most wild area counties to support projected popu-
> lation growth in those counties for the next 100 to 300 years.
> A typical county, Madera, has seen 21,048 lots bulldozed in
> the past 20 years, but only 100 houses now sit on these lots.

Developers have been gobbling up California's open spaces
at a rate of between 50,000 to 100,000 acres annually, yet
structures have been built on only 3 percent of all recreation
lots sold in recent years. As the Nader report said, the
California situation has many "similar parallels throughout
the country." In New Mexico, for instance, the Central
Clearing House, a conservation group, estimates that subdividers have platted enough lots to house more than 2
million people. Colorado's State Lands Commission says
there are twice that many homesites in that state alone.

Indeed, no government agency or individual can even guess how much of the countryside in the United States is being chopped up by these tremendously profitable ventures. One company alone, the Boise Cascade Corporation, a huge conglomerate, has developed or is developing more than 200 square miles of virgin land in 30 projects in a dozen states.

The ravages of fast-buck subdividing have been particularly startling in New England. In Vermont, a land of dazzling green hills and breathtaking mountain vistas, more and more countryside is being turned into what Governor Deane C. Davis calls "a manmade jungle" by uncontrolled development.

So many developers — more than 100, by the best reckoning — swarmed into Windham County, Vermont, a few years ago that land prices rose. With the rise in prices there was an increase in taxes, and some residents had to sell their farms because they could no longer afford to live there. Few of the developers there have ever heard of even the most rudimentary site planning. Because impermeable bedrock underlies much of the soil, septic tanks frequently overflow, spilling wastes into lakes, streams, or a neighbor's well.

The specter of similar pollution has caused officials in Pennsylvania, where an estimated 800 recreational lot developers are active, to break out in cold sweats. "If the scores of new communities planned by developers in the Poconos ever materialize, those mountains could become an open sewer with people drinking water contaminated by their own wastes," says Bette Clemens, former director of the state's Bureau of Consumer Protection and later an official of the Council of Better Business Bureaus, Inc. "This area is being emasculated by developers who know that the soils are not suitable for on-site sewerage and water systems. Yet they sell lots in the area with only token mention of the sewage problem and make no provision for a central system." Because of high density soil compaction most Pocono Mountain land is unsuitable for septic tanks. "People could be swimming in lakes fed by septic tanks and they could be living along roads which could be potholed night-mares," Bette Clemens said. Pennsylvania's State Health Department has reported cases all over the state in which people paid thousands of dollars for lots but could not build on them because their applications for septic tank permits were rejected.

In Manchester, New Hampshire, banker Paul Leaming remarked that many artificial lakes devised by recreation lot developers "have turned into mud holes where you'd probably get typhoid if you swam in them. Not only that, but all sorts of friction occurs when 500 people try to use two tennis courts and a 20- by 40-foot clubhouse."

Secretary of the Interior Morton, in testimony before the Senate Interior and Insular Affairs Committee in 1971, said: "Manmade lakes — from Barecroft and Occoquan in Virginia to Lake Mead behind the Hoover Dam — are silting up. And the mineral content of the waters we drink and use for every purpose is changing. On parts of the Colorado River scientists of the [U.S.] Geological Survey have calcu-lated that salinity is double what it was when the river ran free."

Said the Nader report: "When all the [selling] ballyhoo has subsided, the lots sold, and the developer departed, what is the residue? Public access is lost to lakes and streams by lots that are owned but not used. The land is frequently badly scarred by roads and fill, and natural ground cover is permanently devastated. The courses of streams are purposely altered. Wildlife habitats are bulldozed into ex-tinction, and the damage to flora and trees begins the natural cycle of damage to wildlife."

In Virginia certain large-scale developments are exerting "a significant adverse impact" on the environment, concluded a special environmental study conducted in 1971 under the auspices of the Governor's Council on the Environment. In several parts of the state environmental quality is "critically impaired or challenged" already by "ill-planned" developments, said the report, submitted to Governor Linwood Holton. Declaring that Virginia's land use policies are "grossly inadequate," the report recommended the establishment of effective safeguards and the creation of firm guidelines for planning and land use priorities.

The waters of Lake Tahoe in California's Sierra Mountains are being polluted, perhaps irretrievably. "Man's potential for destroying the beauty of Tahoe must be recognized and controlled — now," insists Charles Goldman, a University of California limnologist who has studied the lake's progressive deterioration for years. "Every disturbance of the watershed has its influence. . . .The erosion rate continues to increase with every form of land disturbance."

Incline Village, a Boise Cascade project on the Nevada side of the lake, was stalled for more than a year when environmentalists, belatedly awakening to the dangers threatened by this and dozens of other developments, imposed increasingly severe safeguards.

In far too many developments roads are not maintained and thus fall into ruin. During rainy spells they turn into torrential sloughs. In mountain areas or foothills the resulting erosion can be devastating. A case in point is Shelter Cove, on the fogbound California coast north of San Francisco. When heavy rainstorms caused washouts in the 4,700-lot development, the county discovered that road construction was below prescribed standards. The county road engineer estimated in 1970 that two thirds of the roads were unacceptable and that it would take $2 million to bring them up to standard.

Subdividing is "one of the most destructive forces at work on today's forests," said Edward F. Martin, chairman of the southern California section of the Society of American Foresters, when he testified before the Senate Committee on Interior and Insular Affairs in 1971. "There are countless examples of this in southern California, where forested mountains have become high-elevation extensions of the urbanized megalopolis. Drainage patterns are being severely upset since

20 percent of the land surface in developed areas is covered by streets and roofs. Air pollution is choking trees — the very trees which cleanse the air.

"Indiscriminate subdivision development has greatly increased fire hazards to forests and at the same time increased the potential for loss by complicating fire-fighting efforts," Martin said. He also declared that more than 60 percent of the nation's "most productive forest area is in fragmented farms and other small ownerships subject to serious developmental pressures which are destructive to the forest environment."

Underground water tables in some areas are being drained so heavily that springs and streams are drying up and sea water is seeping into wells. It has happened in south Florida, where the ground water has sunk to alarmingly low levels and large stretches of the Everglades are in jeopardy. On the fringe of adjacent Big Cypress Swamp developers have dug drainage canals that lowered the water table from two to four feet.

Moreover, the booming growth of the land sales industry has increased the perils to both land resources and consumers. In order to maintain sales volume and profit margins land companies must continually subdivide new properties. With scores of huge corporations now in the business, the competition is more intense than ever. As the competition grows, salespeople are more pressured to stretch the truth.

Authorities in some areas are, fortunately, awakening to such dangers. Bills are pending in Congress that would, for the first time, establish a national land use policy, and many states have begun to consider remedial legislation.

Prodded by environmentalists, the federal government has moved on several fronts to halt assaults on natural resources. It has been proposed, for example, that the government should buy 547,000 acres of Big Cypress Swamp and preserve it as a national recreation area. In 1971 President Richard Nixon declared that such action is necessary to protect the area "from private development that would destroy it" and, in the process, destroy much of southern Florida's water supply and the Everglades National Park.

There is strong and growing national sentiment behind such actions, but the fight to curb profligate development will be long and difficult. The land sales industry is influential, affluent, and well organized. Most significantly, subdividing land is still one of the easiest ways to make a fast buck.

5

The Boom in the Boondocks
— Second Homes

U_{NTIL} the mid-1960s, the interstate land sales
industry was composed primarily of companies offering retirement homesites and "investment" property in Florida, several
western states, and a few foreign countries such as Brazil and the
Bahamas. Then, around 1965, the business swelled to un-
dreamed-of-dimensions. The catalysts were twofold: the growth
in the market for the recreation or second-home development
and a fever of land speculation (see Chapter 6).

Developers suddenly discovered a huge untapped market for
recreation-oriented properties of every description. Second-
home communities, mountain retreats, ski resorts, and camp-
grounds began sprouting up like daisies on a spring meadow.
Newspapers, television screens, and billboards burst forth with
seductive advertisements.

Newsweek reported in 1968: "So swiftly is the second-home
market expanding that statistics can't keep up with it." *Business*

Week predicted the following year that "one-fifth of all houses built annually during the next 10 years — some 200,000 to 250,000 — will be mountain cabins, seashore cottages, and desert retreats." The *Wall Street Journal* said in late 1970, "Although overall housing starts this year will actually lag behind a decade ago, recreational home starts will be up 150 percent." In 1971 the American Land Development Association (ALDA), a trade group composed mainly of leisure-time property developers, estimated that the annual rate of recreational land sales — excluding dwellings — had reached $5 billion. ALDA calculated that if the average lot cost $8,000, developers were selling well over 625,000 lots a year. The National Association of Home Builders (NAHB) estimated that 95,000 second homes were built in 1971, up from 90,000 in 1970, and predicted that the yearly total would reach 130,000 by 1975.

A combination of forces is behind the surge in land sales. The fundamental factor, of course, is rising affluence. Since World War II the United States has enjoyed its most prosperous years in history. As the United States entered the 1970s, Americans on the whole had higher incomes and more savings than ever before. Per capita purchasing power was at record levels despite the effects of inflation. The average family income was expected to reach $12,500 or more by 1975, up from $9,200 in 1968.

Added to increased wealth are the growing disenchantment with urban living and the availability of more leisure time. Vacations are longer, life spans are stretching, and many workers are retiring earlier. Modern cars and highways have made it easier to "escape."

"Second-home owners want . . . their leisure surroundings to look as unlike their everyday neighborhoods as possible," the National Housing Center Council (NHCC) has noted. "They want their children to have trees to climb, chipmunks to feed, mossy banks to climb, berries to pick." As one lot-hunter, Mrs. John Dewees, of Winston-Salem, North Carolina, wistfully put it: "I don't want much. Just so we have a view, a stream, and some rocks. . . ."

Others want more than a change of scene, and developers have eagerly accommodated them with such amenities as golf courses, beaches, marinas, community centers, tennis courts, riding stables, parks, and stocked fishing lakes. The rage of leisure-time developers in recent years has been the planned community encircling a manmade lake, an idea pioneered by Thomas J. Perine, chairman of United States Land, Inc., of Indianapolis, a company that was acquired in 1967 by the Boise Cascade Corporation.

U.S. Land starts by finding a rural valley, preferably near a city, fed by a fresh-water stream. Across the stream goes an earthen dam. As the water backs up to form a lake, bulldozers cut in roads, building sites, open-space areas, and golf courses. Meanwhile a massive promotional campaign is launched and a high-potency sales force goes to work hawking lots.

In its first such undertaking, Holiday Lakes, near Cleveland, Ohio, the company sold nearly all of the 1,270 homesites in two months. Then came Lake Holiday, near Chicago, Lake of the Four Seasons, near Gary, Indiana, and others. U.S. Land's sales volume shot up from $1.5 million in 1964, its first year, to $30.5 million in 1967, when it was taken over by Boise Cascade. Boise approximately doubled that figure in 1968.

Its acquisition of U.S. Land, plus some smaller companies, made Boise Cascade the largest developer of recreational real estate in the nation. Land development meshed neatly with Boise's other activities. The company, based in Boise, Idaho, is engaged primarily in the manufacturing and marketing of forest products but has diversified in recent years into building materials other than lumber, paper, publishing, packaging, office supplies, factory-built houses, on-site houses, apartments, and mobile homes. Its president, Robert V. Hansberger, has negotiated more than 35 mergers since taking over the helm in 1957. The company grossed $1.7 billion in 1970 and, in terms of total assets, was listed thirty-fifth from the top of *Fortune* magazine's rankings of the largest U.S. corporations. To handle its land development activities Boise formed a new subsidiary, Boise Cascade Recreational Communities, Inc.

"Boise Cascade is concerned with self-image and is relatively honest in salesmanship," the Ralph Nader task force commented in its 1971 report on land use and power politics in California. The *Wall Street Journal* asserted in 1970 that "Boise . . . is considered more responsible in its marketing than many developers."

Laurels notwithstanding, in 1971 the state of California and Contra Costa County filed a suit accusing Boise Cascade of using misleading representations in the sale of $46 million in lots between 1967 and 1969 in four development projects in Calaveras County. The suit asked damages of $2,500 for each misrepresentation, $1 million punitive damages, and restitution to allegedly defrauded purchasers. Named as defendants were three Boise subsidiaries — Boise Cascade Home & Land Corporation, Boise Cascade Credit Corporation, and Boise Cascade Recreation Communities, Inc.

When the action was instituted, Judge Robert Cooney, of the Contra Costa County Superior Court, issued a restraining order prohibiting the subsidiaries from engaging in deceptive practices. He also directed Boise to place all past and future profits from sales of land in the four developments into a trust and said that no foreclosures against purchasers would be permitted.

In Alameda, California, a lower court jury awarded two Boise customers $43,331 in restitution, then slapped the company with $500,000 in punitive damages after agreeing that a salesman had misrepresented Boise property. Boise officials termed the verdict "absurd and unsupported by the evidence"; they said a new trial will be sought.

How could a company of Boise's stature get into such difficulties? Company officials claimed that, for one thing, Boise Cascade's size and visibility have made it a natural whipping boy for environmentalists and consumer-protection groups. Another problem, admitted Vice-President John Fery, was that the company inherited a good many irresponsible managers and high-pressure salesmen with the companies it acquired. "We had people running the operations who didn't give a damn about Boise Cascade's public image," Fery fumed.

One of the projects that Boise took over after its 1967 merger with U.S. Land was Lake of the Woods, a 3,800-lot development 70 miles south of Washington, D.C., in the rolling hills of central Virginia. During an 18-month period more than 3,400 persons paid between $4,900 and $30,000 for property in that area. All through 1967 and 1968 Washington-area newspapers and television stations made Lake of the Woods household words. "Come where all the action is," blared radios and televisions. "To big, blue Lake of the Woods!" And thousands did.

Indeed, high-voltage selling is the key to second-home property sales, just as it is for peddling desert "homesites" and Florida swampland. Thus in addition to high-pressure on-site selling (with two-way radios, cracker-jack salesmen, etc.) Boise Cascade and other companies use cocktail parties, dinner parties, free gifts, and newspaper and television ads to woo prospects. One spokesman said that U.S. Land and its successor, Boise Cascade, spent $10,000 a week promoting Lake of the Woods.

U.S. Land's stunning success quickly attracted scores of competitors. *Business Week* reported in 1970 that more than 50 major corporations were involved in some form of leisure time development; the roster included the St. Regis Paper Company, Union Camp Corporation, Westinghouse Corporation, Scott Paper Company, Ford Motor Company, General Electric Company, Alcoa Corporation, the Weyerhaeuser Company, International Telephone and Telegraph Corporation, Inland Steel Company, Transamerica Corporation, Dart Industries, Inc., Tenneco, Inc., Avco Corporation, CNA Financial Corporation, International Paper Company, Walt Disney Productions, LTV Aerospace Company, and Signal Oil Company.

According to the ALDA's reckoning, more than 10,000 developers were active in 1971. Nobody knows the actual total, however, and the number of developments is far larger than that. American Realty Service Corporation, for example, has built no fewer than 54 projects in 20 states. Boise Cascade counted 35 in 1971.

While second-home developments come in every description imaginable, the formula perfected by U.S. Land is one of the most commonly used. A developer buys up several thousand acres of unimproved land for between $200 and $800 an acre, gouges out some roads, stakes off areas for an artificial lake, a clubhouse, a golf course, and various other facilities (to be built later), and starts selling. After the last lots are sold, most developers pull out, leaving the community in the hands of a property owners' association. Occasionally such a group will encounter unexpected problems such as uncompleted streets or an unpaid mortgage. In 1970, ten persons who bought property in a Calvert County, Maryland, vacation development charged in a federal suit filed in Baltimore that improvements were "largely nonexistent" after ten years of promises.

The plaintiffs, who claimed to represent lot owners in 12 states, demanded $5 million in damages from the White Sands Corporation and agent Effries M. Freeman of Lusby in Calvert County. Their complaint charged that the 700-acre tract was still largely woodland and that some of the lot buyers had been unable to locate their property. No roads had been built, but fees for road construction had been collected, the plaintiffs said.

Even when a developer leaves things in good shape, property owners often have their hands full. "Who knows anything about running a community of several thousand people?" asks a Federal Trade Commission lawyer. Contractor Gayle T. Dorman likewise points out, "Without a builder around, people don't know where to turn. They find themselves in all kinds of difficulties."

Dorman should know. His company, Mountain View Homes, Inc. (he is vice-president), is associated with John D. Flynn, Jr., in the development of Shenandoah Farms, in northern Virginia, 70 miles from Washington, D.C. In ten years this Blue Ridge Mountain resort blossomed from a wilderness into an attractive $6 million-plus community of middle-income second homes. Of the 2,000 persons who bought lots during that period, more than 400 built secluded retreats among high mountain slopes or along the winding Shenandoah River. Others use their lots for weekend camping in tents or trailers. Along with clean air, majestic vistas, and serenity, property owners can avail themselves of such activities as swimming in heated pools, fishing, hiking, and horseback riding.

Shenandoah Farms doesn't favor dinner parties or super-charged selling, and its prices reflect the low promotional costs. Half-acre lots averaged $2,800 in 1970 (up from $1,000 in 1960), and it was possible to buy a new three-bedroom riverfront home — including lot and plumbing — for less than $15,000.

Flynn credits the development's success in large measure to the presence of a builder who operates all year 'round on the premises. "A builder is essential, especially in a somewhat remote area," he asserts.

Dorman adds: "If lot buyers don't build, the land just sits there." In the early 1970s Dorman was putting up dwellings — everything from $4,000 chalets and A-frames to $35,000 luxury homes — at a rate of about 70 a year.

Unlike Dorman of Shenandoah Farms, most developers of recreation communities prefer simply to sell lots without waiting around to build. The ALDA estimates that only about 200 firms throughout the United States specialize in second-home construction, whereas the number of subdividers probably exceeds 10,000. When miniscule lots bring $4,000 to $30,000 each, companies with big national sales networks ideally can make $10,000 or more per acre. (For example, at Lake of the Pines, located in California's Nevada County, land was purchased for $873 an acre and sold a year later for $12,000 to $36,000 an acre.)

Business is not always that good, of course. Toward the end of the 1960s the industry found itself in a heavy thicket of difficulties: attacks by environmentalists, tougher restrictions by local planning authorities, rising construction costs, and tight money. These troubles, together with the 1969-1970 recession, resulted in a shakeout that left some outfits liquidated and others faced with a profit squeeze. Boise Cascade, which in

1968 had confidently talked in terms of an "apparently insatiable" demand for second-home lots, saw its sales plunge from $209 million in 1969 to $158 million in 1970 as a direct result of a precipitous drop in land sales. Its land sales subsidiaries caused the company so much grief in the form of declining revenue and horrendous publicity that, according to published reports, the company came perilously close to shedding all of its land development operations. Boise announced that it would no longer engage in the practice of selling lots for their purported investment value, but whether salespeople can be prevented from doing this is questionable.

In 1971, with the recession ended and consumers starting to spend more liberally again, some of the clouds began lifting for the developers. As these words are being written, there is every indication that recreation lot sales will continue to be buoyant for some years to come, yet there are clear signs of market saturation in some areas. "It's a problem in the sense of developing an oversupply, even to the point of glutting," said Burton F. Smith, a former real estate commissioner in California, where 50,000 to 100,000 acres of rural lands were subdivided annually in the latter part of the 1960s and early 1970s by recreation lot developers. This amount accounted for nearly 25 percent of the state's subdivision activity and added up to nearly $250 million a year in estimated market value. By 1971, however, houses had been built on *only 3 percent of the lots sold* in the previous decade.

To illustrate what was happening the Ralph Nader study gave the status of several of Boise Cascade's California developments, which were described as "typical of the rest of the recreational subdivisions in the state." Lake of the Pines had 1,944 lots with 100 houses at that time. Ranch Calaveras, covering 5,200 acres, had 9 houses, 8 of them models. The Circle XX Ranch had nothing but gravel roads spread over 3,200 acres. The two houses at Woodland Hills Country Estates, a 2,700-acre tract in the San Fernando Valley, were occupied by Boise executives. "Mountain Meadow, near the town of Tehachapi, has 2,000 acres with eroding dirt streets, and one lone ranch house which is used as a sales headquarters," Nader's investigators said.

Lake Los Angeles, 15 miles east of Palmdale, had 4,500 lots with 25 houses, "all of them built by the developer to stimulate interest," the report continued. Lake Don Pedro, in Tuolumne and Mariposa Counties, consisted of 12,000 acres and an enormous "hacienda," which serves as a sales office and is planned as a future country club, plus a few scattered houses. Pine Mountain Lake, in Calaveras County, "consists of 3,500 acres and a filled-in artificial lake." The Nader investigators found "a similar absence of construction at Lake Wildwood in Nevada County, an area of . . . over 3,500 lots."

The report said that "a single proposed development in Shasta County would house its entire population. Within the last 20 years, 21,048 lots have been offered for sale in Madera County. This would house Madera's entire population many times over. As with Shasta and most of the counties here listed, existing lots (if used for living quarters) could accommodate the established growth rate for the next 100 to 300 years."

If ALDA's estimate of recreational lot sales and NAHB's second-home estimate are correct, lot sales are exceeding house starts by 530,000 a year. Undoubtedly some buyers will build eventually, and others want the lots for campsites or status symbols. Still, there is every reason to believe that millions of lots will remain vacant for generations. Why? Because well over half of them, according to surveys of some developments, are bought for speculation. The industry owes much of its spectacular growth to the ability of salespeople to convince millions of people that buying lots is a great way to invest money.

A federally funded study of Brooktrails, a development on California's northern coast, found that 78 percent of the buyers considered investment potential one of the main reasons for buying; recreation was listed first by only 23 percent.* A poll of

*The survey found also that most buyers were married couples with children and were employed in white- or blue-collar jobs paying between $10,000 and $20,000 a year. The average age of purchasers was 40.

lot owners at Lake of the Pines indicated that nearly 70 percent bought principally for "investment and resale."

Many developers ballyhoo the investment angle harder than the delights of leisure living. "Have you noticed that practically every big rich man plants his money in real estate?" booms the sound track for a film shown by American Realty Service Corporation. "Rockefeller made millions and planted it in real estate. The Vanderbilts, the Carnegies. . . . In fact, do you know any big rich man who doesn't own real estate? What better way to invest your money? The Department of the Interior said in 1967 that land prices increase 15 to 20 percent a year. Everywhere you look you'll see land values climbing up, up, up! Wouldn't it be wise to buy land somewhere — anywhere — before prices get out of reach?"

That kind of razzle-dazzle may sound a little crude, but it works.* And salespeople occasionally get an assist from the press. "The appeal of the second home is not entirely a matter of pleasure seeking," *Newsweek* told its readers in 1968. "Soaring land values alone make many acres an attractive investment. . . ." The *Wall Street Journal* commented in 1970: "With resort area land values rocketing, the investment motive ranks high with many second-home buyers." Two months later, however, *Journal* reporter A. Richard Immel did an in-depth analysis of troubles afflicting the recreation land industry and reported, in part: "Critics also worry about speculation in the lots once they are sold. . . . Salesmen have often wooed buyers with promises of quick killings to be made in resale. In many cases the resale market disappears as fast as the sales force."

In the Lake of the Pines poll, conducted by Nevada County District Attorney Harold Berliner, two thirds of the 1,000 respondents said they would not make such an investment again. Half of those had already put their lots up for sale but did not expect to break even. Within three years after purchase 42

---

*The persuasiveness of some salespeople is almost beyond belief. In July, 1971, the *Washingtonian* magazine, in Washington, D.C., published an article exposing high-pressure sales tactics of several developers in surrounding areas. The writer, Diane Shah, and her husband posed as prospective buyers at several projects in the course of the investigation. Later she confided to me: "You know, we actually came close to buying ourselves at a couple of those places."

families had lost their property by foreclosure, and only one lot had been sold for a profit.

At Virginia's Lake of the Woods only 107 building permits had been issued by the end of 1971. There are 3,800 lots in the development. Since the sales force broke camp, hundreds of purchasers have listed their lots for sale with real estate brokers or in classified newspaper ads that, more often than not, contain such statements as: "$100 cash and take over payments" ... "Must sell" ... "Sacrifice" ... "Any reasonable offer considered" ... "Will sell for 1968 price" ... "Below cost."

A few phone calls to advertisers turn up one hard luck story after another. An army officer reassigned to Vietnam must sell within five days or risk the loss of his $2,000 equity. A young couple with three children and unexpected expenses will gladly accept $3,500 for the $4,500 lot they bought "at an impulsive moment" three years before. A federal government employee transferred to St. Louis offers a $500 discount and adds: "If that's not enough, make me an offer." An older couple has a "once in a lifetime" opportunity to buy a farm for retirement in Maryland; they need $6,400 in additional cash and will gladly take that for two $5,200 lots at Lake of the Woods.

Besides the difficulty of finding people with ready cash, lot sellers find themselves competing with scores of other developers. There are nearly one hundred leisure-time developments within 100 miles of Washington; several were started after Lake of the Woods. In fact, Boise Cascade launched another project, Ocean Pines, 150 miles away, in Maryland. What's more, all of the major developers in Florida and the Southwest maintain powerhouse sales forces in the Washington area. Residents are bombarded with a constant stream of dinner invitations through the mail, over the telephone, in newspapers, and in television commercials. The same situation prevails in many urban centers.

A lot owner who tries to sell through a realty broker is likely to find dozens of such listings already on file. Brokers "already have thousands of listings for development property," says Don Miller, a Rehoboth Beach, Maryland, real estate dealer. "Why should they push your lot ahead of anyone else's?"

A few owners have managed to unload by arranging a deal with a salesperson at the development. Usually they offer the salesperson a 15 or 20 percent commission instead of the 10 percent normally paid by developers. Of course, this method ceases to work once the sales force pulls up stakes.

Too, many families have been skinned by developments that went under, such as the Four Seasons resort near Newnan, Georgia, and Parker East near Denver, Colorado.

A number of second-home developers have been embroiled in battles with environmentalists or owners of neighboring property. In 1969, for example, Boise Cascade bought 17,000 wooded acres along a finger of Puget Sound near Bremerton, Washington, and set about converting a third of the property into a community of vacation homes. When the company failed to give assurances that it would install a sewer system, conservationists and local residents organized a protest movement, and the Kitsap County Commission imposed so many conditions that the project was halted.

At Incline Village, an incomplete resort on the Nevada side of Lake Tahoe, Boise Cascade was given the title of "polluter of the year" by a group of students. The company's request for permission to construct 3,000 homes was greeted with furious opposition by conservationists, who accused Boise of scarring the forests and contaminating the lake with silt. By the end of 1971 Boise had succeeded in erecting only a handful of dwellings and four condominiums. "We'll never go to a spot of natural beauty again," said the president of Boise Cascade with weary resignation. "The situation is just too emotional." Several Boise Cascade projects in other locations were likewise either shelved or abandoned because of local opposition.

Taxpayers occasionally are forced to foot part of the bill for improvements that benefit private developers. One example is Bryce's Mountain Resort, a popular skiing center and vacation development near Bayse, Virginia. A number of prominent people own second homes there, including former Secretary of Agriculture Orville Freeman and television newscaster Roger Mudd. Out of the forested land at Bryce's was scooped a 44-acre bowl that, in conjunction with a dam, will provide a 1¼-mile lake for the exclusive use of property owners and their guests. The construction will cost about $330,000, and some 78 percent of that amount will be paid by the U.S. Department of Agriculture. The dam is one of more than 6,000 that the department has built to control flooding in small watersheds, and officials declare such construction necessary and desirable. But U.S. Representative Henry S. Reuss (D-Wis.), chairman of a House subcommittee on conservation and natural resources, attacked the project, calling it one of a type that is giving a "windfall" to land speculators.

"Seems to me we are going to have a taxpayers' revolt in this country pretty soon if the average fellow who pays federal income tax finds that his money is devoted to enrich speculators and that he can't even dangle a worm in the water or go swimming on a hot August afternoon," Reuss told the Agriculture Department's Soil Conservation Service, the agency involved.

No conflict has been more acrimonious than that which has swirled for years around Charnita, a $12-million vacationland in Adams County, Pennsylvania, ten miles southwest of Gettysburg. Launched in 1966 by Charles G. Rist, a former tool- and die-maker from Baltimore, Maryland, Charnita consists of 6,500 acres of former farms, forests, and orchards that have been staked out into half-acre homesites costing $3,500 to $15,000 each (compared with an average price of $300 an acre for farmland in the area at that time).

Charnita, Inc., the development company, installed skiing facilities, lakes, a golf course, a clubhouse, tennis courts, and swimming pools and aggressively prospected for buyers through newspaper advertisements, mass mailings, dinner parties, and offerings of free vacation accommodations, trading stamps, gifts, and cash bonuses. By 1972 approximately 5,000 individuals had bought lots, and about 350 homes had been built (including the $150,000 residence of developer Rist). "Property owners . . . enjoy this beautiful, peaceful mountain retreat where the air is cool and clean," gushed Charnita's ads. "They enjoy sparkling lakes fed by mountain streams, good fishing, boating and water skiing. . . ." On the other hand, critics charged that what Charnita and its neighbors would actually end up with would be unprocessed sewage spilling over fields, polluted and silted streams and wells, and countryside rendered useless for building or farming.

In January, 1970, a group of 60 neighbors formed the Tri-Township Citizens Association and squared off for what came to be known as the "Second Battle of Gettysburg." Using ecology as its battle cry, the association filed a series of lawsuits against Charnita, Inc., and lodged complaints with local governing bodies and state and federal regulatory authorities.

At about the same time four lot owners instituted a class-action suit against Rist, charging that they had been victims of fraudulent advertising and selling techniques.

In a statement outlining its purposes and objectives, the new association said, in part: "At this very moment, raw unprocessed sewage is draining into the creeks, mud by the tons washes into the lake every time it rains, and septic tanks are overflowing into the meadows. The whole big mess washes down into Tom's Creek, which is a tributary of the Potomac River. . . . There is no sewage system nor water supply system, although 85 to 90 percent of the land was found by a Pennsylvania geological survey to be unsuited for development with septic tanks. Indeed, the same study declared that such development endangers the ground water supply of the whole area. Nevertheless, the land was sold as suitable for septic tanks and individual wells on each half acre, and parts of it are now developed with houses that have septic tanks. The result is pollution of both soil and water. About 60 miles of rough roads, constructed without regard for soil conservation, cause heavy silting."

The association charged that its complaints were initially rebuffed by nearly every agency, attributing this to what it called the "considerable" political influence of the Charnita Corporation. But in 1971 the Federal Trade Commission found the company guilty of violating the section of the truth-in-lending law that gives buyers who intend to build permanent residences on their lots a 72-hour period in which they can cancel the purchase. The Pennsylvania Department of Environmental

Resources banned further construction of homes in Charnita except where percolation tests showed that septic tanks could be used. Because the ground in those sections cannot readily absorb water, state sanitation engineers prohibited county and township offices from issuing septic tank permits in about 85 percent of the development.

The U.S. Department of Housing and Urban Development (HUD) accused Charnita, Inc., of excluding minority groups; that case was settled when the company signed a consent order agreeing not to discriminate in the future.

In one of its early victories the association persuaded the Office of Interstate Land Sales Registration (OILSR), the HUD division that polices land developers, to compel Charnita, Inc., to inscribe warnings about the septic tank ban on the front cover of its property reports. A few months later, however, the developer was permitted to move the caveat to the bottom of the last page of the reports. Members of the association contended that the change resulted from political pressure; they noted that Pennsylvania State Senator George N. Wade, chairman of the Senate Appropriations Committee, is chairman of the board of Charnita, Inc.

The fight has been punctuated throughout by charges of political machinations, payoffs, threats, slander, and unethical dealings. Local County Judge John A. MacPhail drafted Charnita's incorporation papers. The company's lawyer, Thomas Pyle, is prosecutor for Adams County, where Charnita is located. A member of the board of supervisors for Liberty township, John Flenner, charged in an affidavit that Rist had threatened him with bodily harm when he refused to vote with the other two board members in approving new sections of the development for sale.

Dagmar Perman, one of Charnita's most spirited adversaries, said the developers had branded her as a Communist. Rist, in turn, filed a libel suit against Mrs. Perman, her husband, the association's chairman, William Brent, and his wife. The developer claimed that he was maligned in a letter of complaint that the two couples had sent to former Pennsylvania Governor

Raymond P. Shafer. Excerpts from the letter were published by the *Gettysburg Times*.

The Permans, who live in Chevy Chase, Maryland, a suburb of Washington, D.C., own a 40-acre farm adjoining Charnita, where they spend weekends and vacations. "Our environment has been ruthlessly spoiled," charged Mrs. Perman. "They [the developers] have done everything to avoid their responsibilities."

Brent, who owns an apple farm near Charnita, expressed fears that the development will cause permanent environmental damage and that he, like some of his neighbors, will be forced to sell his farm for additional subdivision development. "They are destroying this valley," he said.

Rist and other Charnita supporters angrily denied that the development is a blemish on the landscape. Many Adams County residents who do not own property nearby viewed Charnita as generally beneficial to the area — at least in a financial sense. In Liberty Township, where 65 percent of the development is located, Charnita represents a potential increase of several million dollars in the tax base. However, there has been no corresponding increase in actual tax revenue because the lots, on which Charnita, Inc., pays taxes until the contracts are paid off, are classified in the meantime as agricultural property and have very low assessments. In time Charnita could indeed produce considerable tax money, but its contribution could be equaled or exceeded by costs of governmental services to the development.*

Charnita's opponents point out that the tax income would soon diminish or stop altogether if the ban on new construction were to be made permanent. They predicted that if lot owners were barred from building on their property, they would stop

---

* The Nader study noted: "Developers like Boise Cascade have deterred opposition [to their proposed development] by developing intricate systems of pecuniary reward for public officials. In cases where the developers run up against an incorruptible public official, they can often still prevail by using their domination of information about the project to argue that the development will increase the local tax base and improve local services. The truth is that these developments often incur greater local government costs in the long run than they bring in local tax revenue."

paying taxes. As an example of what might happen they pointed to Loch Raven, a Rist development in York County, Pennsylvania. The county board of supervisors ordered a moratorium on new construction there and sued Rist on charges of failing to comply with local subdivision regulations. Many lots at Loch Raven were abandoned by purchasers, and "For Sale" signs cropped up on many others.

Rist has always insisted that Charnita is a boon to the area. "I'm being harassed by a half-dozen nuts," the developer told Ronald Kessler of the *Washington Post* in 1970. The following year he was quoted by Michael K. Burns of the *Baltimore Sun* as saying: "I'm very proud of this project. I'm going to live here."

In March, 1972, a personnel shakeup took place at OILSR, and one of the new regime's first acts was to order an indefinite moratorium on all lot sales at Charnita because of Pennsylvania's continued refusal to issue building permits. It was a precedent-setting action. The agency also directed Charnita, Inc., to offer cash refunds to 158 persons who had recently bought lots; the property reports they had received omitted certain information.

But the Second Battle of Gettysburg is far from over. Charnita's ultimate fate may not be known for years. The state of Pennsylvania appears firm in its resolve to ban further construction unless sewage facilities are provided, and there is no certainty as to when, if ever, that might be. "No precise date or time can be indicated as to when a municipal or central sewage system will be constructed," said Charnita's property reports.

Elsewhere, however, the boom in the boondocks rolls on.

6

The Truth about
Soaring Land Values

THE phenomenal growth of interstate land sell-
ing has been generated to a large degree by developers' claims
that people of average means — millions of them — can make
money by speculating in building lots or small tracts of acreage. Developers say that land values are shooting up, and in-
stallment-plan investment programs make it possible for the
little man to get a piece of the kind of action that only the
wealthy could afford in the past. Buy a lot today and sell it in
just a few years for a hefty profit, the spiel goes.

On the surface the proposition may seem attractive. An astute
land investment can indeed pay off handsomely. "Since World
War II," *House and Home* magazine asserted, "land speculation has created more millionaires than any other form of business investment." The first Marshall Field, who made much of
his $100 million in land speculation during the late nineteenth
century, remarked: "Buying real estate is not only the best way,

the quickest way, and the safest way but the *only* way to become wealthy."

Salespeople maintain that in these times of economic uncertainty land investment schemes have distinct appeal. Inflation keeps chipping away at the dollar, bank deposits may actually lose purchasing power because of the living cost spiral, and the stock market has been erratic. Government savings bonds pay relatively low yields; corporation bonds usually produce a better return, but they are unwieldy for small investors.

On the other hand, the salesperson says, land is appreciating fast. Land ownership has always been an excellent hedge against inflation. Since offerings of most installment or interstate land developers must now be registered with the federal government under a new consumer-protection program, the family bread-winner would be wise to put his or her extra dollars into land instead of — or in addition to — stocks, bonds, life insurance, mutual funds, or savings accounts. And the pitch goes on.

But land salespeople seldom, if ever, mention the following facts:

1. Only a fraction of the nation's land — land that can be exploited, largely urban growth-area land— is rising sufficiently in value to make it worth considering as a speculative investment. Most land is not appreciating in value — or appreciating very little — because it is in areas where there is little demand for land.

The popular belief that land values are zooming *just about everywhere* is a delusion. Moreover, even if raw land were appreciating uniformly, the fact would be irrelevant insofar as many promotional lot offerings are concerned.

Raw acreage and subdivided lots are two quite different things, roughly comparable to the difference between orange groves and oranges. The land on which orange trees grow may be priceless, yet the value of a season's orange yield will be low if there is a bumper crop. There is indeed a bumper crop of building lots in many places, and the crop keeps growing.

2. Speculating in land is one of the riskiest and most difficult of ventures. Amateurs should avoid it. Few nonprofessionals

have the time, the knowledge, and the expertise to do it successfully.

People who make money in land speculating almost invariably buy *large tracts* of undeveloped but usable acreage in anticipation of population needs; then they sell it years later or subdivide it into building lots. Speculators in *lots* usually have several things working against them: they pay a premium price to begin with, plus interest if the deal is financed; they not only pay the promoter a profit but they also contribute to the promotional costs, which may add 40 percent or more to the price of the lot (somebody has to pay for all those dinner parties, phone calls, sales commissions, and fancy brochures).

Until the contract is paid off — which may take ten years or longer — the buyer's cash is tied up. As a rule the buyer gets no deed until the last payment is made. The contract can't be freely traded like shares of stock or cashed like a bond. Chances are that if one or two payments are missed, the seller can cancel the agreement and keep everything that's been paid as "liquidated damages." If the seller fails to make promised improvements in the subdivision or cannot deliver a clear title, the buyer has little recourse except to bring costly and often fruitless litigation. As was previously noted, the seller may all the while be subdividing more lots.

When the buyer finally does get a title, there are taxes and maintenance expenses to pay. If the lot should be sold through a real estate broker, the buyer will have to pay a commission of at least 6 percent of the selling price — plus closing costs and possibly legal fees.

If the developer goes broke, lot buyers could lose their equities or never get the promised improvements.

The Urban Land Institute, a research and educational organization based in Washington, D.C., calculates that land must double in value *every six years* to justify holding it as an investment.

Yet according to the Federal Housing Administration (FHA), it took ten years — not six — for the average U.S. homesite to double in value in recent times.

A breakdown of homesite price trends is provided by the National Association of Home Builders (NAHB). Here are some examples:

	1960	1969	% Increase
Albuquerque, N.M.	$2,805	$4,065	45
Birmingham, Ala.	$3,582	$5,451	52
Boston, Mass.	$3,694	$9,210	149
Chicago, Ill.	$4,769	$9,847	106
Denver, Colo.	$4,106	$5,877	43
Jacksonville, Fla.	$2,576	$4,926	91
Miami, Fla.	$3,368	$7,828	132
Minneapolis, Minn.	$3,079	$7,240	135
Orlando, Fla.	$2,453	$4,896	99
Phoenix, Ariz.	$2,766	$4,852	75
St. Louis, Mo.	$4,877	$7,027	44
West Hartford, Conn.	$4,098	$9,915	132

Bear in mind that the figures shown are not costs of second-home lots in the boondocks. They are costs of fully improved (with sewerage, water, and paved streets) sites for new homes in metropolitan centers, where land values are rising the fastest. Note also that in most places the prices did not double even in ten years, let alone six. In many cases the increases in price reflected increases in the size of homesites.

Since New Mexico is one of the areas in which promotional land companies are especially active, let us figure how an investor would have done had he bought a typical homesite in Albuquerque, purchasing it in 1960 for $2,805 and selling it in 1969 for $4,065.

Let's assume that our buyer put $805 down and paid the rest in monthly installments for six years at 6 percent interest. The interest charges would have come to $386. Say that taxes totaled $500 and insurance and maintenance — grass-cutting and the like — cost $250. That brings the total carrying charges to $1,136. The total investment, then, would be $3,941 — compared with a selling price of $4,065. But our investor's costs could be higher than $3,941. When he sells the lot there are closing costs such as transfer taxes, recording charges, possibly even a lawyer's fee. If the sale is made through a real estate broker, the broker will charge a commission of 10 percent of the selling price — $405 in this case.

So our investor could end up losing money instead of making it. If the investor does make a small profit, the dollars received would be worth 28.1 cents less than the dollars used for the down payment and the first year's installments. Inflation knocked that much purchasing power off the dollar during the 1960s.

3. The government's regulatory program provides only limited protection to investors. It has failed by a wide margin to eliminate phony or unfair offerings — as we shall see in Chapter 11.

4. There is abundant evidence that many, if not most, offerings of lots in promotional subdivisions are *worthless* as speculative investments.

The investor who tries to sell may find himself competing not only with the developer who sold him the property but with any other developers operating in the area. In Florida, for example, an individual who tries to sell a building lot competes with such folks as the ITT Community Development Corporation, General Development Corporation, Deltona Corporation, GAC Corporation, AMREP Corporation, and numerous others — plus the countless other individuals who bought lots in the past and are trying to sell them. In New Mexico an individual seller has Horizon Corporation, AMREP, and others as competitors. Similar situations prevail in many places, particularly in large metropolitan areas, where second-home communities abound.

The whole system of promotional lot selling frequently operates to the investor's disadvantage. All too often the buyer pays a grossly inflated price for a piece of ground that may never be resold. Real estate authorities and investment counselors repeatedly warn against speculating in lots, but their words of caution are usually drowned out by the thunderous hoopla of promoters. "Investment in vacant land is full of pitfalls and is subject to such erratic and often unforeseeable factors that investors who expect a safe and quick profit are warned to avoid this field altogether," declares Homer Hoyt, a Washington, D.C., land economist. J. R. Hoffman, former Vice-President of the Council of Better Business Bureaus, Inc., asserts: "Anybody who attempts to make money by speculating on one or two lots is very likely to be disappointed."

Some promotional offerings may contain locked-in impediments to development that are not apparent to people who are unfamiliar with the complexities of real estate investing. Lots may be sold with no improvements other than a network of dirt access roads. Who will make the property habitable? Who will pave the roads, install water and sanitation facilities, put in gas, electricity, telephone lines, and other prerequisites to community living? A salesperson probably will say that contractors will grab up sections of the subdivision to build houses on as soon as the flood tide of people begins. But why should the builders do that when they probably can buy raw acreage a lot cheaper and subdivide it themselves — without having to deal with numerous distant owners?

One would expect that, if homesites were so lucrative for small investors, companies that sell them would go out of their way to compile a track record of how their customers have fared. This would make an impressive sales tool, just as the performance records of the better mutual funds are their biggest selling point. However, if the truth were known about how lot buyers make out, a good many land companies would collapse. A salesperson who is asked for such information will deftly change the subject, say that the company hasn't been in business long enough to establish a record, or tell you that the figures can't be obtained. (The last is an outright lie; prices of real estate transactions can be determined from public records.)

One company, GAC Properties, Inc., did try to develop evidence of price gains. GAC gave up, however, after finding that resale prices of lots at Cape Coral, its most advanced development, rose an average of only 10 percent in ten years.

The salesperson may whip out an imposing chart purporting to show how the *prices* of his lots have risen through the years, but those price changes were made by the company. This old and effective sales gimmick makes it look as though values are soaring. What the charts don't tell is whether any previous buyers have been able to *sell* at those prices — or at any prices.

The Horizon Corporation makes boasts such as these in newspaper advertisements: "You can make money here even if you can't spell Albuquerque," and, "How a very small investment can earn you more than your savings for a whole lifetime of hard work." But Horizon's chairman, Joseph Timan, told the Los Angeles Society of Financial Analysts in January, 1972, that "as yet, a secondary market has not been created for the sale of these properties."

Nobody knows exactly how many people have been skinned on speculative lot purchases, but the number is enormous. In the 1960s Indian Lake Estates, a development near Lake Wales, Florida, went bankrupt, and 3,500 lots were auctioned off. They brought an average of $500 per lot, as opposed to prices of $2,750 and up that were paid by individuals who had bought similar lots in the development.

A revealing situation developed recently at Rio Rico, a 55,000-acre (86 square miles) development in Arizona being promoted by GAC Corporation, the conglomerate that acquired Gulf American Corporation. The tax assessor of Santa Cruz County valued lots there at an average of about $1,600, considerably below GAC's asking price of $5,000. GAC challenged the assessments, claiming that the lots were really worth only $185. At a hearing held by the Arizona State Property Tax Appeals Board, GAC said that the $5,000 price included $2,500 in sales expenses and costs of future improvements.

The improvements, GAC admitted, would not be completed for ten years. Lot buyers may have to wait considerably longer than that for the place to fill up since Rio Rico occupies twice as much ground as San Francisco.

Too, in a large number of cities are to be found real estate dealers from whom subdivided property can be obtained for a fraction of the current price charged by the promoter.

Of course, many things can be bought at bargain prices if you shop around, but that's rarely true of things that are bought as *investments*. Nobody in his or her right mind will sell you General Development stock or gold or rare antiques or mutual funds for less than their prevailing price.

No business inspires more myths and misconceptions than real estate. One of the most cherished beliefs is that Peter Minuit, the Dutch settler, became the all-time champion wheeler-dealer when, in 1626, he bought Manhattan from the Indians for $24 in beads, trinkets, and bright cloth.

Peter didn't do badly; Manhattan's land and buildings are now worth $40 billion. But when the *Wall Street Journal* credited him in 1970 with pulling off "the real estate coup of the age," several readers took exception. One of them, Robin Carpenter of St. Petersburg, Florida, pointed out that:

"For a $24 investment to grow to $40 billion in 344 years, it need only appreciate at the rate of about 6.5 per cent a year. Most investors in real estate (or any other capital-growth speculation) would not have anything to do with such a stagnant situation."

7

By the Acre
or the Gallon

Nine miles west of Daytona Beach, Florida, is a soggy wilderness in which snakes, alligators, and frogs have propagated since the dawn of civilization. Swamps, ponds, sawgrass, scrub oak, pine trees, and dense growth stretch over mile after endless mile of flat landscape. Much of the area is flooded during rainy periods.

Unlike the Everglades, some 200 miles to the south, the place is neither a tourist attraction nor a refuge for exotic wildlife. It is a nondescript patch of the boondocks, typical of vast reaches of inland Florida.

Years ago the section was known as Deep Creek Ranch; a sluggish stream winds through it, and a few of the drier spots were used for grazing cattle. For a long time the owners tried to sell out, but there were no takers.

In 1962 Firstamerica Development Corporation, of Hollywood, Florida, bought about 16,000 acres of the property (25 square miles), paying an average of $180 an acre. The purchase was financed with a $1-million loan from the Teamsters Union pension fund. Before long Firstamerica was reselling the land in small parcels — ponds, creek, and all — for $690 an acre, plus 6 percent interest on installment contracts. The buyers were schoolteachers, physicians, factory workers, clerks — people from many walks of life.

By what magic of merchandising was this feat accomplished? Firstamerica did not drain the property, build roads to the little tracts, or do anything else of consequence to enhance values. Nobody discovered oil, and no important building projects were announced in the area.

The company applied a simple land selling formula with dazzling success — then and now — by many land companies in Florida and other states. First the one-time ranch was presented with a new name — University Highlands. Next Firstamerica splashed newspapers around the country with advertisements offering 1¼-acre tracts to investors as "a rare profit opportunity." To people who responded to the ads Firstamerica rushed lavish multicolored brochures that described the land as "a perfect setting for potential investment profits."

Reinforcing the brochures was a bustling "boiler room" in Hollywood — an office packed with high-powered telephone salespeople who burned up the lines day and night with calls to prospective buyers.

University Highlands is one example of what is called "acreage subdivision," or "investment acreage" promotion — subdivisions in which small tracts of raw land are sold with no improvements at all. Years ago sharp operatives discovered that it was possible to sell land this way simply by convincing distant buyers that the property would jump in value, allowing them to sell it at a profit. There are literally hundreds of such offerings in Florida and many more in some of the western states. Remuda Ranch Grants and River Ranch Acres, Gulf American Corporation offerings, are archetypical examples.

Firstamerica's activities, however, are typical of the usual methods of operators, and if Firstamerica's land is unimpressive, the same cannot be said of its credentials. Fuller Warren, Florida's governor from 1949 to 1953, is a vice-president; his face graces the covers of University Highlands brochures, and a glowing testimonial by him recommends the property to investors. The late T. Frank Hobson, former chief justice of the Florida Supreme Court, was a Firstamerica vice-president, and he is still listed among the officers in some of the company's sales literature. The president of Firstamerica is Frank S. Cannova, former assistant state's attorney-general and former assistant state's attorney for Florida's 15th Judicial Circuit. Among other officers and major stockholders are another former judge, a past president of the Hollywood Bar Association, and a former agent of the Internal Revenue Service.

The company was formed in 1959. Its sales director during its formative years is better known to law-enforcement officials than to the public. He is Dory Auerbach, a Miamian who pioneered in swamp selling and then went west for more grandiose endeavors. On a remote prairie in Mohave County, Arizona, he gave birth to Lake Mead Rancheros and sold "homesites" for $10 a month and up.

"The Rancheros are livable now," screamed ads in major newspapers. "They're laid out, waiting for people. A new community coming to life. You can own a king-sized western estate with ROADS AND ELECTRICITY, WATER AND PHONES AVAILABLE . . . BUILD NOW AND MOVE IN!"

Actually, said J. Fred Talley, the Arizona real estate commissioner, "a bulldozer merely cut scars across the desert, and the developer gave them fancy names." Power and telephone lines were six miles away from the nearest lots, and the only water source — a pipe that jutted out of the desert floor and operated only when a quarter was dropped in a slot — was 12 miles distant. Talley assailed the offering as "the most flagrant [example of misrepresentation] this department has ever encountered."

Mr. Auerbach and two associates were convicted on 22 counts of mail fraud in 1968, after they had sold more than 3,500 tracts at a loss to the public estimated by chief postal inspector H. B. Montague at $1.8 million. Auerbach was fined $10,000 and sentenced to one year's imprisonment. The prison sentence was suspended. One of his partners was fined $7,500 and the other, $5,000. Neither was jailed.

Had Auerbach stuck with swamp selling (he apparently left Firstamerica in 1962), he might never have run afoul of the law. It may not be apparent at first glance, but there is a fundamental difference between Lake Mead Rancheros and promotions like University Highlands. At Lake Mead lots were advertised and sold as *homesites* — places where homes presumably could be built. At University Highlands tracts are sold as *speculative investments* — parcels that, according to the promoters, may be resalable at a profit some time in the future.

The ads for Lake Mead said that the homesites could be lived on, and the courts held this to be a falsehood since utility services were not available within a reasonable distance. The ads for University Highlands imply that tracts there will be in demand as building sites, and while there is no assurance that the land could be built on, regulatory authorities in Washington and Florida have held that such representations are permissible as long as promoters state that the property is sold for investment, that it is not "presently suitable" for development, and that the sellers plan no improvements.

University Highlands was not Firstamerica's first venture. In 1960 officials of Orange County (Orlando) discovered that 1,880 of the wettest acres for miles around were being sold under the name of Orange County Acres — in violation of the county plat law. The Board of County Commissioners took an unprecedented step: it ordered that letters be sent to all known buyers telling them of the property's condition.

The seller? Firstamerica. When the company found out about the letters, president Cannova and vice-president Warren showed up at a County Commission meeting to object. After all, argued Cannova, ads for the property made it clear that the tracts were being sold for investment and that no improvements were planned. The commissioners retorted that the offering was deceptive because the land could not be used without costly improvements.

The commissioners threatened to sue. "You try to make us feel that we're committing a crime," Cannova protested.

"We think you are," one commissioner shot back.

Snapped another: "Would you gentlemen please get out of Orange County and not come back?"

Warren and Cannova did precisely that. In neighboring Volusia County the company found a friendlier political climate, and there it concentrated its subsequent operations. In just 87 days the company sold all 3,500 lots in a watery jungle called New Smyrna Acres. West Daytona Acres, which is 22 miles west of Daytona Beach, also sold well.

In the case of University Highlands Firstamerica persuaded the Volusia County Commission to grant an exception to its otherwise rigid subdivision regulations and allow a plat of the property to be recorded at the courthouse. This curious favor enabled Firstamerica to describe the land as "a platted, recorded subdivision," implying that the area was ready and waiting for hordes of land-hungry developers.

In another clever stroke Firstamerica talked the West Volusia Zoning Board into rezoning a square mile of the tract for industrial use. That section was christened the "Nova Industrial Park," and the 1¼-acre tracts within it were represented as industrial property. Although no substantial improvements were made or contemplated, salespeople hawking tracts in other parts of University Highlands could say: "You know, a big new industrial park has been established right on our land!" But new troubles lay ahead. The possibility that thousands of lot buyers might try to settle on the property alarmed many of the county's residents. At a series of public hearings held by the West Volusia Zoning Board, Dr. Robert O. Vernon, director of the Florida Geological Survey, and others testified that the drainage of surface water could deplete vital underground fresh water reservoirs that feed wells all over the county. To forestall such a misfortune the board zoned a 60,800-acre area, including University Highlands, as a water conservation district, with land usage restricted to agriculture except where a valid case for special exemptions could be made. This was a stunning blow for Firstamerica; it meant that the property could no longer be represented as a future metropolis without risking fraud charges. The Florida Real Estate Commission, which censored advertising for such promotions in those days, stood ready to ban all references to development in University Highlands ads.

"An unwarranted abuse of authority," roared George Polera, Firstamerica's vice-president-in-residence, in assailing the zoning board's action. "They can't do this!" When cries of indignation brought no response, Polera called on the board's attorney, William E. Sherman.

"He advised me that Firstamerica intended to file suits against each of the five individual zoning board members — as individuals — for acting in excess of their authority," Sherman related later.

The board members stood their ground, confident that the costs of defending any such actions would be paid by the county, as was customary. Then three of the five county commissioners indicated that they would not authorize a defense. "We thought they were overstepping their authority, and when you think somebody is overstepping their bounds, you don't go ahead and defend them," said Harris Saxon, who was then head of the commission.

Commented Sherman: "I would think that any public body defends it employees and officers until such a time as it is clearly shown that they have acted beyond the scope of their authority." Noting that no litigation had even been filed, Sherman said the board members would not have lost the suits, but "It would have cost them thousands of dollars to defend them."

On June 6, 1962, the zoning board members resigned, an action that nullified the water conservation zoning. Firstamerica proceeded to excavate a five-mile-long drainage canal, and while the facility has never served any function except to illustrate University Highlands brochures, it prompted demands from several civic groups that the area be protected. Lee H. Maxwell, who had been chairman of the defunct zoning board, made speeches around the county calling for conservation measures, but he fell silent when he was again threatened with a suit for damages. Soon afterward he lost a bid for reelection as president of the county Democratic Club.

Other odd events occurred. The county engineer, Wesley Sweat, who had made critical remarks about University Highlands and had balked at signing the plats, suddenly resigned without explanation. H. Deane Smith, a county building inspector who had investigated the company, was fired. Wendell L. Richards, chief county sanitary engineer, was called into his superior's office after he denied a request for a letter authorizing the use of septic tanks in University Highlands. There sat George Polera and two county commissioners, Ralph Richards and Grady Williamson. "Just their appearance indicated they were trying to put pressure on me," he said afterward. Still, the letter wasn't forthcoming.

In 1963, however, public pressure became such that the county commission finally agreed to order an engineering study to determine the consequences of draining the recharge area. This was done by the U.S. Geological Survey at a cost to county taxpayers of $150,000. The findings? The area is in fact a vital water source. Since no development has taken place, however, the reservoir remains intact.

Nothing really can stop a company's sales spiel. The 20-foot-wide canal to this day has no outlet, but it provides another helpful sales aid. It is prominently pictured in the brochures and labeled "The Grand Canal." The original brochures carried a letter by William E. Swoope, Jr., a land surveyor from nearby New Smyrna Beach who had done some surveying for Firstamerica. "This property is, in my opinion, suited for development of homesites, business sites, and industrial plant sites," the letter said, in part. "A portion appears suitable for citrus production." Inclusion of the letter had not been authorized by the Florida Real Estate Commission. Only through an inquiry from a prospective purchaser did the commission discover that Mr. Swoope's observations were being circulated far and wide. They were promptly ordered to be stricken.

There are good reasons to doubt that the property will ever be developed at all. As we have seen, geologists and conservation experts have testified that draining or paving over the property could destroy water sources that supply homes over a 50-mile radius, including those in Daytona Beach.

Even if that weren't a problem, the difficulties facing tract buyers would be formidable. In order to have any value at all land must be usable. Putting the University Highlands tracts to a use that would appreciably increase their value — such as for residential and commercial building sites — would require extensive improvements.

Drainage alone could cost millions of dollars — the water table is just two or three feet below the surface — and there is no assurance whatever that such a project would be feasible, either economically or physically. Parts of the property may be too mushy for building anyway. When Interstate 4 was built through a corner of the area a few years ago, contractors encountered muck pockets 30 feet deep that had to be dredged and filled. A county health officer described University Highlands as "low-lying, marshy and submarginal . . . unfit for residential purposes until suitable and necessary drainage has been established." Indeed, as required by law, Firstamerica's sales material states — albeit inconspicuously — that no improvements are planned.

No developer, of course, would spend millions of dollars for reclamation when plenty of high, dry, usable land is available for much less money than the tract buyers paid, especially since if anyone ever did wish to take on such a project, the developer would have to find, contact, and negotiate with hundreds or thousands of owners living all over the world in order to assemble enough land for a subdivision. Moreover, many of the tract buyers did not receive rights to any oil, minerals, or other valuable deposits that might be found.

Those rights were retained by previous owners. Consequently, getting a building loan from a bank or savings and loan association would probably be impossible; mineral rights permit the holder to drill or excavate on the property.

These problems however, have not come within several light years of eliminating mass sales of low-grade or unusable land. Swamp selling is still a major industry in Florida, with numerous offerings similar to University Highlands. In May, 1970, a full year after the federal law took effect, the *St. Petersburg Times* reported that the business had reached such colossal proportions that "It's posing a threat to the public interest of all Floridians."

Florida is not the only place where poor-quality acreage is sold to distant investors at fantastic prices. In several of the western states promoters have prospered from sales of desert wastes, dry gulches, gullies, mesas, and mountainsides. In Sun-West Acres, an Arizona subdivision, it would cost each lot owner more than $10,000 to install a well and up to $10,000 more to extend electric lines ("if the electrical company deems such extensions feasible"), according to public reports that the sellers must furnish to California residents. At Whispering Pines Estates, in Deschutes County, Oregon, the cost of putting in a well and pressure system could exceed $2,000. Ocean View Estates, a subdivision in Hawaii, is near two active volcanos. During one of several volcanic eruptions lava flowed directly through the subdivided areas.

In Florida the swamp peddlers have their own trade organization and lobby — the Florida Land Association — to which approximately 150 corporations belong, according to its founder and general counsel, Miami Beach attorney Morton Rothenberg. The association's president is Fuller Warren, and its vice-president is M. Howard Webb, former president of Webb Realty Corporation, a pioneer swamp seller with a rare gift for candor. Years ago he advertised: "Buy it by the acre or the gallon!" In 1969 Webb Realty was sued by a customer, who charged that he was sold land within a flood-control easement — a fact that was typed into the contract after he signed it. The man won the case. Webb Realty and three other corporations headed by Webb were acquired in 1969 by Nortek, Inc., a diversified company based in Providence, Rhode Island. Webb still heads several other corporations.

Another of the Florida Land Association's directors is Sam Sacks, a Miami Beach real estate broker who in 1969 was convicted of mail fraud in the selling of unimproved desert as homesites in an Arizona subdivision called Arizona Ranchettes. Sacks was fined $7,500 and given a one-year prison sentence, which was suspended. Sacks later appealed, and his case was dismissed.

Other charter members of the association include the Canaveral International Corporation, a diversified concern (transportation, real estate, etc.); the Florida-Collier Acreage Corporation; Florida Sunland Acres, Inc.; Miami Gulf Land Investors, Inc.; Mr. Land, Inc.; Collier Land Investment Corporation; Florida Ranchettes, Inc.; and Cape Canaveral Corporation.

Few swamp merchants who have strayed beyond what the law allows have been prosecuted, but in almost every case the prosecuting was done by agencies outside Florida. One of the star witnesses at U.S. Senate hearings on the truth-in-land-sales bill in 1966 was Fred Fogarty, then real estate editor of the *Miami Herald*. To the amazement of members of the Committee on Banking and Currency, Fogarty gave an account of how several enterprising people had bought land in a flood-control district in western Dade County for $45 an acre and were selling it to northerners for $240 an acre under the name of Golden Palm Acres.

The land, Fogarty testified, is in "a water storage area for the Everglades National Park. They hold water back, and when the park becomes dry, they gradually release it into the park to sustain all of the wildlife." This information was not divulged to buyers.

SENATOR WILLIAMS: If anybody buys an acre in Golden Palm, he might be high and dry one year and under water the next year?

FOGARTY: That is true. I would say that he would be under water both years.

SENATOR MONDALE: Did the State of Florida do anything to prevent this?

FOGARTY: No. To my knowledge they haven't done anything. . .

Florida authorities had known all about Golden Palm Acres because the *Herald* had published a detailed article about it by Fogarty seven weeks before the Senate hearings.

In the glare of national publicity the U.S. Department of Justice obtained mail-fraud indictments against several persons involved with Golden Palm Acres. In 1969 Louis Pilnik, the corporation's president, was sentenced to two years' imprisonment. Salesmen Allan Harris, of Irvington, New Jersey, and Rubin Ehrlich, of New York City, each drew one-year terms.

In an unrelated case New York state authorities obtained $359,341 in restitution from the Cavanagh Leasing Corporation, of Miami, for New York residents who had been induced to sign contracts for the purchase of real estate through promotional contests (in which nearly everyone was a "winner").

In 1972 a New York court ordered Nortek, Inc., to refund some $15,000 to New Yorkers who bought lots in Rainbow Park, Interlachen Lake Estates, Collier Land Investment Acres, Crescent Shore Heights, and Forest Lake Campsites. Another company, Corporation of Americas, Ltd., signed a New York consent order in which it agreed to repay $338,000 to buyers of lots in Cape Kennedy Estates, Cape Atlantic Estates, Lake Harney Ranchettes, Ocala Thoroughbred Acres, Mount Plymouth Golf Estates, and Miami West. Both firms had failed to register their offerings in New York state and obtain permission to sell there.

Over the years New York has forced developers to refund hundreds of thousands of dollars to New York residents. Many Florida offerings are barred from New York. The state has a tough land sales law, one of the best in the nation, which prohibits the sale of offerings deemed unfair. But some New York citizens get taken anyway.

New York will not authorize sales to its residents of lots

that are under water, inaccessible by car, or otherwise unusable. The state contends that such offerings are inherently unfair. After a large tract of land is subdivided and sold to thousands of distant buyers, who will make it habitable? Who will provide drainage, build roads, install water and sanitation facilities, put in gas, electricity, telephone lines, and other prerequisites to community living?

The inevitable result of such subdividing is a "legal wasteland," asserts Robert Doyle, former planning director for the East-Central Florida Regional Planning Council. "Subdivisions of the fast-buck variety usually produce land utilization problems for almost everyone associated with such projects other than the initial promoters," Doyle declares. "As is often the case, there are no available funds to provide the necessary improvements, and thus individual building efforts are stymied and the land lies dormant."

California Assistant Attorney-General Herbert E. Wenig told the U.S. Senate subcommittee on frauds and misrepresentations affecting the elderly that "the sale of undeveloped lots in a premature and remote subdivision for use as homesites or investment is inherently fraudulent." He cited the same reasons that Doyle had given.

Such sales flourish because the profits are fabulous and because government regulators in most jurisdictions have refused or failed to control the selling of land. The builder of a livable community must put out large sums for streets, sewers, and other basic improvements. To attract customers such bonuses as a golf course, marina, clubhouse, or community swimming pool may be added.

The desert peddler or swamp merchant has few, if any, of these costs. For as little as $5,000 or $10,000 down a developer can gain possession of hundreds of acres, often with options on more. With cash from installment sales the note can be paid off and the options picked up, with perhaps additional profit. The swamp seller needs no surveyor; the tracts are sold by unmarked legal descriptions, known as "metes and bounds."

A dramatic case history of such difficulties was compiled

when Walt Disney Productions, Inc., acquired the property for Disney World, 12 miles southeast of Orlando. The $5-million, 27,000-acre tract, high and dry for the most part but with several swampy areas, was assembled for the Disney firm by Nelson Boice, Jr., a real estate broker and president of Florida Ranch Estates, Inc. Putting together that much land is seldom easy, but this project was complicated enormously by the fact that parts of the area has been sold off in small parcels by acreage promoters. The purchases of the parcels had to be shrouded in secrecy lest word get out that Disney was interested. Had there been any errors, Florida might have lost what promises to be the biggest single economic bonanza in its history.

Boice and members of his staff — all of whom had been pledged to secrecy — worked five or six nights a week for *two years* before a sufficient number of parcels was in hand to induce Walt Disney to proceed with the project. Even then many purchases could not be negotiated. The average price paid was $185 per acre.

"To be blunt about it, some of the owners had been swindled," says Mr. Boice. "Their lots were miles from passable roads and were inhabited only by rattlesnakes and alligators."

Swamp selling has attractive tax advantages as well as low overhead. A subdivider can usually qualify his property for rock-bottom agricultural assessments by, for example, grazing cows on it. One outfit rents a few heifers just before assessment time and returns them a few weeks later.

It is unlikely that many of the hundreds of thousands of swampy acres that have been sold in Florida will ever be used for anything. Thanks to relentless pressure from environmentalists, the state has suddenly become ecology-minded. Two multimillion-dollar federal projects that had been energetically pushed by segments of the business community (a huge jet airport in Miami and a barge canal cutting through the center of the state) have been abandoned because of the threat they posed to natural resources. Developers once had virtually a free hand in carving up the countryside and dredging canals; today their plans are getting hard-nosed scrutiny in Tallahassee.

Despite successes in many areas of sales control, efforts to discourage swamp selling have met with relatively little success. Florida's regulatory authorities have long contended that such offerings are legal and proper so long as buyers are informed in writing of the land's physical condition, the terms of sale, and certain other facts. In accordance with state and federal laws such information must be disclosed in printed prospectuses, or property reports. As seems to be the rule in land sales reform, however, the enforcement of laws is still more problematical than the passage.

8

Some Tricks of the Trade

P_{HONY} research reports, irrelevant statistics, booby-trapped gift offers, "free" lot gimmicks, bogus vacations, bait-and-switch advertising, doctored contracts — you name it, somebody has used it to peddle land.

Land hustlers have no monopoly on wiliness, of course, but many of them employ certain specialized techniques and stratagems that work especially well in the selling of subdivided land. The most common ones are:

The Money-Back Guarantee. Nearly all subdividers whose properties are sold sight unseen give a refund privilege, a high-potency selling point. "What have you got to lose?" the salesman demands to know. "If you don't like the land when you see it, you'll get every penny back."

It seldom works out that way. Contracts usually stipulate that the money will be returned if the buyer personally inspects the property within a specified period of time — usually six months — and finds that it was misrepresented in any way. The

123

catch is that proving misrepresentation is extremely difficult and costly, if not impossible. In fact, the cost of traveling to the property may well exceed the buyer's equity in it.

Buyers who do make such a trip are met by salespeople who are every bit as overpowering as the one who sold them the property in the first place. Indeed, many people are talked into buying *more* land. A sales manager for Silver Springs Shores, a development in Central Florida, once bragged to the author that "At least 70 percent of the people who come down and look at their lots sign up for more of them."

The Inspection-Trip Refund. Some companies offer to pay all or part of a customer's travel expenses if the buyer inspects the property and agrees to go through with the purchase. Here again there may be strings attached. For instance, a Maryland psychiatrist who visited an El Paso, Texas, development after being told that the company would pick up part of the tab, was told when he got there that the company's portion would be deducted from the *final* payment on the contract.

The Hidden Waiver of "Cooling-Off" Rights. The federal truth-in-land-sales law says that if a buyer isn't given a property report at least 48 hours before the contract is signed, the buyer is entitled to a 48-hour "cooling-off" period after signing. During that time the buyer can cancel the deal for *any* reason, notify the seller of the cancellation, and demand a refund.

This provision could have been a crippling blow to the thousands of recreation lot developers who invite prospects to their properties, deliver a sledgehammer sales pitch on the site, and get a contract signature then and there. Applying their lobbying muscle, the developers persuaded Congress to provide a waiver clause stating that a buyer may give up the cooling-off period by signing a waiver statement. The waiver is ordinarily part of the small print in the contract — usually unknown to the buyer. Simply by signing the contract the buyer automatically gives up the right to cancel. Sometimes the waiver is printed on a second sheet of paper that is handed to the buyer along with a stack of other documents that require a signature.

Inclusion of the waiver clause was an unconscionable capitulation to industry pressure; no purchaser should surrender the cancellation right for any reason. Developers argued that a person who inspects a lot needs no property report, which, of course, is untrue. As the Office of Interstate Land Sales Registration says in form letters it sends to inquiring consumers: "Personal inspection of land will not tell you whether it is fairly priced and will not reveal problems which may exist with respect to such things as the legal title to the property, building restrictions, zoning laws, health regulations, unusual weather conditions, and similar matters."

Concealment of Recision Rights. The federal truth-in-lending law provides an escape clause for some land buyers. A person who agrees to purchase land that might later be used as a primary place of residence may, if the transaction is financed, cancel the deal for any reason within 72 hours after signing the contract. This is called the right of recision. In order to exercise that right the buyer needs only to notify the seller in writing that the contract is canceled.

Recision rights are not given to buyers who plan to use the property for a second home or for leisure-time activities. The right of recision was not included in the law for the purpose of protecting land buyers; it was added to make it tougher for unscrupulous merchants, such as home-improvement racketeers, to bilk people by pressuring them into signing second mortages to finance repairs and foreclosing when they defaulted on payments.

Any creditor who takes a second mortgage or other security interest in a domicile is required to give the buyer a printed notice of the recision right, but subdividers of second-home or investment properties do not have to do so unless they know that a buyer intends to use the lot as a primary residence. However, attorneys for the Federal Trade Commission, which administers the truth-in-lending law, urge such developers to explain the recision right to all buyers. Generally they do so, if only to forestall possible court action by anybody who might subsequently try to cancel a contract on grounds of not having been told.

Many developers fail to inform customers of the escape clause, and occasionally one will answer to the government as a result. For example, in 1971 Charnita, Inc., in Pennsylvania, was found guilty by the FTC of neglecting to tell a number of buyers about this provision. At this writing the case is on appeal.

Sometimes buyers are inveigled into signing away their recision rights under the lending law as well as their cancellation rights under the land sales law. A former salesperson who saw this slick piece of hocus-pocus pulled many times explained how it works:

> Right after truth-in-lending went on the books, the rate of contract cancellations shot up like it never has before. People would go home, start thinking about what they were getting into, and cancel out. So some companies devised a very elaborate form. It's called the "Buyer's Understanding and Declaration."

The form recapitulates several provisions that appear in the sales contract. Between these paragraphs is a statement declaring that the property will not be used for a primary residence. By signing the form the buyer surrenders the recision right. The ex-salesperson explains further:

> When the salesman presents this form he says: "Mr. and Mrs. Jones, I believe you live on Clyde Street, right?" They say yes. "Is that your permanent residence?" the salesman asks. The answer is yes. "Okay, just initial this." The salesman doesn't read it to them.

FTC attorneys say that recision rights continue indefinitely, so a buyer who thinks that he or she has been victimized in this way may still be eligible for legal redress.

The Annual Price Boost. Land companies commonly raise the prices of their lots at frequent intervals, often once a year. This act can spur sales in two ways: it enables salespeople to say: "You'd better buy now; the price will go up on January 1"; and it enables the company to display charts, graphs, and tables showing a steady increase in price over the years. Such sales literature is impressive — especially helpful in talking up lots as speculative investment — but it can be misleading.

The first lots in a new development are usually priced low in order to attract large numbers of early buyers and to allow plenty of leeway for future price increases. In addition, gains that took place during the 1960s aren't as big as they look since price inflation knocked off about 25 percent of the dollar's purchasing power during that decade.

The charts likewise do not take into account the interest, maintenance, taxes, commissions, and other expenses involved in the purchase and sale of a lot. The prices shown do not represent prices that individual owners were able to get by *selling* their lots; they may have had to settle for considerably less — if they could find a buyer at all.

Research Reports and Advisory Opinions. Until recently many of the more unprincipled land companies included "economic letters" or "research reports" with their sales literature. This material, which would boost the company's land or offerings like it, would be produced by the company itself, but it would bear the name of a subsidiary, making it appear to recipients that the material had been written by independent experts on land economics.

Regulatory authorities have put a stop to this practice, but some questionable activities persist. Starting in 1964 Horizon Corporation, the promoter of several subdivisions in the Southwest, distributed hundreds of thousands of copies of a booklet entitled *How to Successfully Invest in Real Estate.* The text strongly plugged properties of the type Horizon offers and indicated that inspecting a piece of property purchased for investment really isn't necessary — a contention that is in direct conflict with the advice of most consumer-protection agencies.

Prior to 1970 nothing in the booklet informed readers that Horizon had underwritten it. Then the New York Department of State, which regulates subdivision offerings, stipulated that copies distributed in New York must state on the cover that verified offering statements, or prospectuses, for Horizon properties could be obtained by prospective buyers on request. Acting on a complaint, OILSR ordered Horizon to insert a statement saying, in part, "A prospective purchaser of land should request a [federal] property report from Horizon Corporation prior to any purchase of land."

Soon after that *How to Successfully Invest in Real Estate* was supplanted by a new publication, *Make Money in Land: A Guide to Successful Investment*, by William Laas, a paperback book published by Popular Library. A price of 95 cents appears on the cover, but the book is sent free to thousands of persons who call for information in response to Horizon's television commercials or who clip and mail coupons that appear in newspaper ads throughout the country.

Make Money in Land does not reveal the author's credentials, if any, and page 4 reveals that the copyright is held by the Horizon Corporation. Chapter 1 is entitled: "Big Profits in Small Lots." Noting that the Federal Housing Administration reported a 95 percent increase in homesite prices in ten years, Laas observes: "Paradoxical as it may seem, choice undeveloped land in the Southwest may have greater potential for percent of profit than a towering New York skyscraper. All depends on where it is and where people are heading."

One is informed later that people are heading in droves to Albuquerque, New Mexico, and El Paso, Texas, where Horizon happens to have huge tracts of land for sale. Curiously, only one land firm is mentioned in the book — Horizon. "Today Horizon Corporation is a publicly owned, nationally known, and respected growth company," Laas writes. "The dynamic growth of Horizon Corporation in a single decade is itself strong evidence of the upsurge of the market for land in well-selected areas of the Southwest."

Laas asserts that Horizon "has been a pioneer in promoting the new-town concept.* Realistically, Horizon president Joseph Timan says, some 300 to 400 such new towns should be started during the next two decades, with or without federal backing."

---

* But not in building new towns. Of Horizon's $78.7 million in sales last year, only $1.7 million came from home construction. Most of the rest was from sales of partly improved and unimproved lots, marketed with heavy emphasis on the "investment" theme. The company's 1971 net profit, incidentally, was $15.6 million, or 19 percent of sales.

In chapters entitled "A Prudent Way to Invest" and "How to Buy Land Now" Laas offers detailed instructions by which people of average means can put their savings in land investments. He argues that new federal and state laws now give land buyers a good deal of protection, adding: "In the homebuilding spree that many economists foresee as the next major phase of America's growth, the value of land can go nowhere else but up."

For the convenience of its readers *Make Money in Land* includes a postage-paid postcard for obtaining more information — from Horizon, of course. What the book doesn't include is a statement informing readers that Horizon paid Laas for writing it.

For the Federal Trade Commission, which has cracked down hard on deceptive advertising in recent years, *Make Money in Land* has posed a singular dilemma. It is being distributed far and wide by Horizon to advertise its offerings, but can it be called advertising? How could the government censor it without infringing on the author's constitutional right of freedom of the press? Even though Laas's opinion may run counter to those of every accredited real estate authority in the country, he has every right to express it. The FTC, which launched an investigation of Horizon and other land companies in October, 1971, has been studying the matter, but it had made no determination when this book went to press.

Altering Contracts. Many land buyers have charged that terms of their contracts were changed after they signed them. They said that somebody erased and changed certain words or figures that had been typed in blank spaces on the form. The commonest complaint was that dates on which the developer agreed to complete improvements were moved back.

Consumer-protection authorities strongly recommend a careful reading of all contract language, preferably by a lawyer.

The Free Vacation. By official estimates about 750,000 persons are lured to Florida annually by vacation offers from developers or contest promoters. The "vacationers" are delivered into the hands of a convoy of high-pressure land salespeople.

The procedure usually works like this:

Patrons at shopping centers are urged to sign up for a "vacation drawing." Entry blanks are passed out from booths plastered with pictures of sun, sand, and palm trees. Prospects are told that it costs nothing to enter the contest, and maybe — just maybe — they'll win a week's vacation for two in "fabulous Florida."

Nearly everyone who fills out an entry blank receives a letter soon afterward congratulating the applicant on winning second prize — off-season motel accommodations in Florida for three days (there seldom is a first prize). By sending in $15 the winner can claim a vacation certificate.

When the certificate comes, the recipient usually discovers that there are numerous strings attached. In most cases the recipient must pay travel expenses and may make the trip only during the summer season, when Florida is usually hot and muggy.

Those who accept the offer are likely to be informed that the motel certificate won't be honored unless the couple (usually only couples are allowed) agrees to tour a land offering and listen to a sales pitch.

Profits from such promotions can be enormous for developers and contest companies. More than two dozen contest promoters originated during the late 1960s, and the competition became brutal. In New York state, for example, the attorney-general's office reported that one Florida promoter employed convicted felons to "use strong-arm tactics" on competitors and on store managers who balked at allowing contest salespeople on their premises.

Lehigh Acres, Inc., in Florida, was hit a few years ago with a civil suit in which the New York attorney-general accused the firm of "fraudulent" and "illegal land promotion" in the use of vacation come-ons. The company signed a consent decree in which it admitted no wrongdoing but agreed to refund $605,852 to New York residents who had bought land after accepting vacation offers.

In 1969 complaints from infuriated "vacationers" became so frequent that Florida adopted a law decreeing that vacation certificates must carry a statement revealing any tie-in with a land promotion. The state served notice that anyone convicted of attracting vacation "winners" to the state under false pretenses would be subject to a $100,000 fine or two years' imprisonment. There have been fewer complaints since then, the state reports, but vacation deals are still a source of irritation.

Some operations apparently didn't get the word about the new restrictions. In November, 1971, the Division of Florida Land Sales of the Department of Business Regulation issued a cease and desist order against Groveland Ranch Acres, Inc., and its president, Stan Rowen, and Holiday Promotions, Inc., and its president, Phillip Gold, ordering a halt to the distribution in several northern states of vacation certificates that had not been submitted to the division for approval.

The Free-Lot Ploy. This is probably the oldest and, until recently, the most widely used scheme of all. A promoter advertises that a lot will be given away "absolutely free" if the prospect will inspect it. The prospect who succumbs to the scheme discovers either that the lot is too small for a dwelling so an adjoining lot is necessary, or that there are certain "incidental expenses" involved in taking title to the property.

Years ago the National Association of Real Estate Boards issued a special bulletin about this stunt:

> The most prevalent method of extracting money from excited "winners" of free lots is to charge them for the "cost of searching the title, drawing the deed, making the transfer," etc. The collection of these sums. . .gives the good-hearted promoter ample profit for his trouble. In most cases of this kind. . .the "incidental" charges were more than the value of the land. For example, in one case. . .the land was bought for $20 an acre, cut up into six or seven lots per acre, and "given away" for $39 title expense per lot.

Another version of this approach employs the bait-and-switch technique. The gull is shown a "free" lot that is miles from the core of the development; the prospect is told that if the location is not suitable a discount will be given on a lot closer in — in an amount equal to the value of the "free" lot.

Misstating Interest Charges. "What's the rate of interest for financing this?" a prospect asks a salesperson. "Only 6 percent," is the reply. Don't be too sure. There are different ways of expressing interest rates, and the actual costs vary considerably.

Land developers frequently charge "add-on" interest. If a salesperson says "6 percent add-on," that means that the amount to be financed is increased by 6 percent, and the buyer pays 6 percent interest on the entire amount. The buyer is really paying 10.9 percent in such cases. On a $10,000 deal the interest cost would be $1,090 — as compared to only $600 for a straight loan at 6 percent annual interest.

Under the requirements of the truth-in-lending law the lender must tell prospective buyers in writing exactly how much they will pay in financing charges and the annual interest percentage. All buyers should check that statement carefully.

Gifts. Developers of second-home lots offer a wide variety of inducements to get people to look at their property — chafing dishes, trading stamps, cash for travel expenses, cameras, fishing equipment, "special discounts" on lots, and various other gifts, prizes, or bonuses.

Many of these offers are legitimate, but the visitor must tour the property and listen to a sales pitch before receiving the items. Usually the gifts are mailed to the prospect weeks after the visit.

Some enticements are completely phony, such as one that drew hundreds of New Jersey and Pennsylvania residents to a Pocono Mountain vacation community near Albrightsville, Pennsylvania, a few years ago. The visitors discovered that certificates for $500 "prizes" they had received in the mail — "payable on demand at Holiday Poconos Estates and Country Club" — were worthless except as down payments on houses and lots. The angry throngs, some of whom had traveled more than 100 miles, were so outraged that state troopers had to be called to the scene to maintain order.

Another near-riot occurred in Pennsylvania when a developer ran out of merchandise that was advertised as prizes. In still another incident hundreds of people swarmed to a vacation development in response to ads for a "sweepstakes" with $40,000 in prizes. The "prizes" turned out to be discounts on lots.*

The Add On (not to be confused with add-on interest). When customers of some land companies miss a payment or two, they are apt to be questioned by a salesperson. If a customer says that the problem is financial, the salesperson will reply: "Well, if that's all it is, I can fix things so your payments will be a lot lower." If the buyer displays the slightest interest in the proposal, the salesperson pulls out a contract form, starts writing rapidly, and says: "You know, you're very fortunate. I just happen to have a very choice lot in the new section we've just opened. It's a *tremendous* buy. So here's what I'm going to do. I'm going to refinance the deal you've got now, giving you *twice* as long to pay. Then I'll give you a long-term contract on the second piece of property. You'll be paying *30 percent less* a month, and you'll be getting *twice* as much land. You understand, I'm only permitted to do this for our good, loyal customers, like yourself. Now, just sign here. . . ." The buyer's payments will be lower, all right, but there will be more than twice as many of them.

Experience has shown that people who have bought land in the past can often be persuaded to buy more land. They are better prospects, in fact, than people who have never bought. GAC Corporation alluded to this fact in classified ads seeking salespeople for its Poinciana development in Florida. The ads, published in early 1972 in several metropolitan newspapers, said in part: "The thousands of GAC property owners in the local area who have property in Cape Coral, River Ranch

* Many people in the crowd came away with something, however. Since there were very few parking spaces at the site, many motorists parked on the shoulder of a public road leading to the model homes. When they returned they found that state troopers had ticketed their cars for illegal parking.

Acres, River Ranch Shores, Golden Gate, Remuda Ranch Grants, and Barefoot Bay in Florida plus Rio Rico in Arizona are all built-in prospects, plus all the millions who will visit Disney World."

The Telephone Blitz. Before disclosure laws were enacted, a large percentage of land sales were made by telephone. The sales volume dropped somewhat as the companies turned more and more to dinner parties and home visits in order to deal more effectively with difficulties posed by property reports and cancellation privileges. But the telephone still is extensively used, particularly by outfits that sell unimproved or partly improved acreage.

In Miami, a major nerve center for Florida companies, scores of crowded boiler rooms hum with activity day and night. Armed with city directories, prospect lists, and type-written scripts, telephone salespeople hunch over partitioned tables, jabbering away incessantly over WATS (Wide-Area Telephone Service) lines.

Boiler room operators maintain tight security; no stranger is allowed beyond a reception room. Job applicants are screened like candidates for the intelligence corps to prevent a newspaper reporter or state agent from slipping through.

Three kinds of calls are made by salespeople — the "front," or initial contact; the "drive," used when a prospect hasn't mailed back a contract and check; and the "load," in which people who have bought before are called again in an attempt to "load" them up with more land. About 20 percent of all load calls result in sales, as compared to five percent of the calls to people who haven't bought before. Salespeople are supplied with leads from several sources: coupons mailed in by people in response to print-media advertising; cards filled out at fairs, shopping centers, or tourist attractions; guests lists purchased from motels; and mailing lists bought from concerns that collect names of car buyers, boat owners, magazine subscribers, credit card holders, and others who seem reasonably affluent.

Scripts used in front calls vary according to what is offered, but most of them have striking similarities. Here are excerpts from a typical one (the name of the company is fictitious):

Greetings and a warm hello from the XYZ Land Company here in Miami, Florida, Mr. _____. How are you today? How's the weather up in your part of the country? My name is Mr. _____, and I'm the national account advisor with XYZ Land.

Have you been enjoying the encyclopedia and the newsletters on Florida land that you have been receiving? Wonderful, Mr. _____. The reason I'm calling is that a very unusual situation and some very exciting news have taken place. You see, Mr. _____, we are making a special test program to see whether or not we can use the phones as a future means of doing business. Naturally, if this is successful, we would be able to save thousands of dollars which normally would have been spent in national advertising.

Quite frankly, I was going to make an offering to you, and it's pretty difficult to turn down if you're interested in making money on a short-term investment — something over the next 12 to 18 months.

Do you have a few moments? Mr. _____, what is your first name? Can I call you _____? Call me _____, and if you have any questions, just cut into my conversation.

As I said before, the land newsletter has recommended this property to their readers as a fantastic investment on a short-term basis, and there are many reasons why they have done this.

You see, XYZ Land is located five blocks from homes selling for between $25,000 and $35,000. It's just 10 blocks from a shopping center. Aerojet General, one of the major companies in the country for the space program, is in the area, and they are planning to employ 20,000 people over the next five years. The growth of Miami has been over 400,000 in population over the past six years, and it's not going to stop now. Properties within five blocks of the area have been selling for $8,000 an acre.

From a price standpoint this is the most outstanding offering I have seen in all of Florida in the past 10 years, and the reason I say this, we are offering at this time an acre and a half — which would break into four giant-size homesites — at just $4,995, financed very comfortably at $50 down and $50 a month.

Now here's the exciting news. Within the next few days we plan on going out to over 250 brokers throughout the United

States with the remaining properties, at which time there will be a $1,000 price increase. Now, how does that sound so far?"

Now in order to protect yourself against the pending price increase, this is what I want you to do. I want you to sit down right now and make out a $50 reservation check and mail it down to the company immediately. Now, understand what this means. It doesn't mean you're buying or making a purchase of any kind. What it simply does is place a hold on the property for 30 days and gives you and the Mrs. plenty of time to go over all the material and come to an intelligent decision.

If you decide you're not interested, drop me a line, or better still, call me collect and back goes your reservation check as fast as it came down. Fair enough?

Do you have a pencil? Take this down. My name is _____. You make the $50 reservation check payable to XYZ Land Co.

Now, _____, I'm getting these papers out to you air mail, and you will get the $50 check out today or at the latest tomorrow? OK?

Now, _____, if you will allow me to be your eyes and ears and advise you and guide you, I'll promise you one thing. When you get down to Florida, you'll have a big box of cigars for me — I'll earn it for you.

It was a pleasure talking to you.

I have listened to at least two dozen phone salespeople in action, and every one was a true master at the hard sell. But the all-time champion was a fellow who worked for Webb Realty Company, of Miami. Webb advertised south Florida acreage extensively during the 1960s, and one day I noticed one of its ads in the *Army Times*. It featured a picture of a Florida pine forest, a coupon, and the words: "For Sale, 5 Acres; Full Price, $795, $10 down, $10 a month."

I was curious, so I mailed in the coupon. In the ensuing four weeks I received *six* calls, all from the same character.

"If ya wanna make money, this is for you," he rasped. "This whole area is gonna boom. You can write your own ticket. This is definitely a blue-chip investment. Prices are definitely gonna jump. We've been swamped with orders. You betcha."

Between calls I made a few inquiries. The advertised five

acres, I learned from officials of Collier County, consisted of unarable rockland and cypress swamp that is flooded at least four months of the year and is ten miles from the nearest settlement — a place called Copeland, population 100.

Tremendous numbers of telephone solicitations are made by sellers of retirement homesites and second-home property, but they are mostly to invite prospects to dinner parties and to make appointments for salespeople to visit them. An idea of the high cost of making a sale can be gained from calculations made by Lewis Berry, the former director of consumer protection for OILSR.

Berry calculated that out of 22,000 calls that are made to set up appointments for salespeople to visit homes about 650 appointments are actually made. These visits result in 300 appointments for prospective buyers to inspect the land. Of these 300 about 90 show up. Approximately 22 of these sign contracts.

That means it takes about 1,000 phone calls to produce one sale.

The Lot-Exchange Privilege. To counter prospects' fears that a lot they select will not be developed when they want to build, most land firms stipulate that a buyer can exchange his property for an improved site or even a lot in another development. This proposition may be legitimate enough, but customers usually find that the improved parcel — if one is available — costs more than the one they bought.

The Buy-Back Offer. Many land buyers have complained that salesmen told them the company would repurchase their property any time they might wish to sell. This is almost always a falsehood; companies rarely if ever repurchase lots from customers.

9

Dinner at Eight

THE most widely used selling device of interstate land companies is the dinner party. Free dinners are to land what supermarkets are to groceries and door-to-door salespeople are to brushes, vacuum cleaners, and encyclopedias.

Thousands of these affairs are held almost every evening in cities and towns across the country. General Development Corporation, ITT Community Development Corporation, Horizon Corporation, GAC Corporation, Boise Cascade Corporation, and hundreds of other companies constantly flood the mails with enticing invitations. Just about everyone whose name appears in a telephone book or a city directory is a candidate for a land sales dinner, although many companies prefer to confine their guest rosters to people in the middle income bracket (mailing lists of people in various income or occupational groups are available from a variety of sources). Thus it is not unusual for residents of some metropolitan centers to receive three or four dinner invitations a week. Some land companies prospect with such a wide net that they find themselves feeding college students, unemployed breadwinners, and consummate freeloaders.

Dinner parties, often called receptions, are uniquely suited to lot selling. They lend a certain dignity to the promotion, and they provide a captive audience, members of which are at least mildly curious about what their host has to offer. After partaking of free food (sometimes preceded by a cocktail or two), watching a movie, and hearing a bewitching sales spiel, some folks are ripe for the kill.

Only a small fraction of such dinner guests end up buying property, however. Lewis Berry, director of consumer protection for OILSR, the federal land sales regulatory agency, has estimated that out of every 270 couples who attend these affairs, 25 sign contracts for lots, and some of those will eventually stop making payments. Even so, a 10 percent selling average is more than enough to justify the enormous cost of party selling. Food and drink aren't the only expense items; the sellers must also mail thousands of invitations and telephone the recipients to confirm reservations.

The dinners are held usually at good restaurants or hotels, and the program is almost always the same. After an opening speech by the head salesman, dinner, and a movie about the development, the guests get a power-packed sales pitch. There are two types of climaxes. If the development being promoted is reasonably close by, the sales force will simply try to get guests to make an appointment to visit the site. The salespeople do this because of a loophole in the federal truth-in-land-sales law (see Chapter 11), which says that any purchaser who fails to receive a federal property report at least 48 hours before signing a contract may demand and get a full refund of any monies paid in — *except* in cases where the purchaser inspects the site in person and signs a waiver of recision rights. Since handing out property reports 48 hours before trying to get contract signatures would kill a lot of sales, recreation land developers make every effort to get people out to the property. At dinner parties where this tactic is used, the development company usually requests a $10 or $15 deposit, refundable if the customer shows at the development, where the heavy selling artillery is used.

If property being offered at a dinner is located in some distant place, the selling team puts on a now-or-never blitz to close sales then and there. Seldom do guests get much, if any, time to read contracts, property reports, or other documents; this really isn't necessary, they are told, because the "money-back guarantee" will make it possible for them to do this at their leisure and still get a refund if they want it. People who leave the restaurant without buying are rarely pursued with follow-up calls, and those who insist on thinking it over are considered lost forever.

"Only one in 10,000 ever comes back," confided Ivan Paul, a sales manager in Maryland for AMREP Corporation's Silver Spring Shores, in Florida. "If you do come back, I'll light a candle in the church." In order to gather research for this book my wife, Ginny, and I attended dozens of land sales dinners, including AMREP's, posing as customers. Ivan Paul spent 90 minutes one evening trying to sell us a $5,400 lot that, he said, was almost certain to double in value in three years. He told us that the lots were selling at such lightning speed that there just wasn't time for reading contracts.

"Oh, come on, now," I replied. "You know nobody in his right mind goes into a $5,400 deal without reading the contract."

"But you get a money-back guarantee. And you know something? Sixty percent of the people who come down and visit buy *more* property."

Paul didn't have to light a candle, but I did go to his office the next day and ask for a blank contract. He cheerfully handed one over but made no further attempt to talk up the lot. Instead he started grumbling about the caliber of land salespeople. "A person who works at it can make good money in this business," he remarked. The proof was right there on the wall — a sales scoreboard for September, 1971. It showed that the people working for Paul had grossed an average of about

$40,000 each. Commissions range between 6 and 7.5 percent, so a $40,000 man got at least $2,400 for about 20 evenings of work. "Good money," said Paul, looking at me intently, "but you can never get enough good people."

The first land sales dinner Ginny and I attended was given by Gulf American Corporation, which pioneered and perfected this mode of selling. It was held in April, 1965, in Daytona Beach, Florida.

We presented ourselves at Daytona's Holiday Inn North. "Gulf American?" inquired a pleasant chap, who introduced himself. "Right this way."

We were, I must confess, a trifle apprehensive. The invitation we carried had been sent not to us but to some friends, and we were using their names. But there was no trouble. The man who greeted us led across thick carpeting to a softly lighted dining room, where another man accepted our tickets without challenge.

"We certainly are glad you could be with us tonight, sir," he said with a broad smile. I thanked him, wondering how long he'd feel that way. Then we were escorted to our table and introduced to two other couples.

No sooner had we exchanged pleasantries than we were joined by a lantern-jawed man who turned out to be a Gulf American salesman. He was called a "land counsellor." Glancing around the room, I noticed that each of the seven or eight other tables also had a counsellor who was setting the stage for the evening's feature attraction with maps, brochures, and contracts.

The evening was filled with exciting talk about money, profits, leverage, courage (displayed by a smart investor who acts decisively on a once-in-a-lifetime opportunity), skyrocketing land prices, booming population, and inflation hedges. But there was little of this during dinner. We were permitted to enjoy our food, and the conversation quickly drifted from real estate killings to other topics.

When the dessert dishes were removed — rather quickly,

I thought — our counsellor got to work. He stood up, peered down at us over his horn-rimmed glasses, and said in a southern drawl: "Is anybody here allergic to making money?"

All heads shook politely in the negative.

"Now, let me make this clear," he went on. "We're not going to sell you anything here tonight. Couldn't if we wanted to. All we can do is accept your reservation."

As it turned out, our host was prepared to accept reservations on a few choice homesites and commercial tracts in Golden Gate, one of Gulf American's developments in southwestern Florida. The reservations could be canceled at any time within six months provided we took a look at the property first. We had to make a down payment that evening, but the deposit would be refunded if we cancelled.

Just then our man was interrupted by a squat, dark-haired fellow who stepped to a podium in the front of the room and introduced himself as a Gulf American sales manager.

The sales manager's name rang a bell. I remembered that he had previously been the local manager for Rocket City, a huge central Florida promotion that went sour and left 2,000 lot buyers in the lurch. "If you think we're going to try to sell you something before we let you out of here, you're right," he boomed, chuckling. In ringing tones he told us how Gulf American had bought up a stretch of wilderness in Lee County, in southwest Florida, seven and a half years before and had transformed it into the thriving metropolis of Cape Coral. The same thing had begun at Golden Gate. Now was the time to get in on the kill.

His audience listened politely, but if they caught his enthusiasm they didn't show it. All of the 29 guests looked like solid, cautious, fairly well off citizens who couldn't easily be conned into anything. Perhaps sensing this, the manager hastened to dispel any fears they might have about buying land without seeing it. Gulf American had become the world's biggest land company in just seven and a half years, he told us. Its sales in 1964 totalled $95 million — "and 75 percent of that came from receptions just like this one."

Next he attacked the problem of economy. If anyone were a

little short of cash at the moment, that shouldn't be a deterrent. "Do you know that 92 percent of the people in America live beyond their incomes?" he asked us.

The sales manager dimmed the lights and showed a color movie of graders and bulldozers charging like a tank battalion through the palmetto-covered flatlands, gouging out water-ways, streets, golf courses, and marinas. When the film ended, he fired up a slide projector. Click! An aerial view of Cape Coral. Click! Happy fishermen on the sparkling Gulf of Mexico. Click! Pastel-colored homes with glittering white roofs. And so on.

Then the manager delivered a primer on land investing. The faces of Andrew Carnegie, Grover Cleveland, Theodore Roosevelt, and other heroes of land development flashed across the screen. A resonant voice told how a few dollars wisely invested with a reputable company can be pyramided into a handsome profit. This was illustrated on the screen with building blocks and simple mathematics in a manner resembling audio-visual aids in a third-grade arithmetic class.

Finally, the sales manager predicted that Collier County, the home of Golden Gate, would "double its population by 1970." (Collier didn't quite make it; its population rose from about 25,000 in 1965 to 36,568 in 1970. The increase from 15,573 in 1960 made Collier the nation's fifth fastest-growing county during the decade, but since Gulf American's successor, GAC Corporation, has well over 50 square miles under development there — enough land to house more than 250,000 people — there should be no shortage of homesites for decades to come.)

When the sales manager sat down, the counsellors swung into action. Our man gave a couple at our table a rapid-fire spiel, but soon he ground to a halt.

"We can't do anything right now," said the woman.

"Why not?"

"Just don't have the money."

"Oh, I've heard that excuse before."

"But it's true. We've had some heavy expenses recently, including a funeral."

"Well, we find that people can always manage to scrape up a

few extra dollars." The counsellor added something to the effect that, if illness struck, money could always be found for doctors. "You've heard that old saying, 'The more you owe, the more you're worth.'"

At that moment a counsellor at another table jumped up and shouted: "Put a hold on lot 112-A!" A murmur of excitement rippled through the room.

"How about it?" demanded our man urgently. "Afraid we can't," the woman replied firmly. She and her husband quickly decamped. The other couple at our table took advantage of the opportunity to leave too. That left Ginny and me exposed to the full force of the counsellor's onslaught. We got a brief reprieve when the sales manager returned to the microphone and said: "Ladies and gentlemen, I almost forgot. With us tonight are a couple who were among the first buyers in Golden Gate, and they're so enthusiastic about it that we invited them back for another free feed. Perry, what do you think of Golden Gate?"

In the back of the room a man got up and said: "Great, just great. That land is already worth twice what we paid for it. And we're gonna buy more. You betcha."

"Let's give them a big hand," the sales manager cried out. The audience clapped indifferently. Later I learned that the man was a Gulf American salesman who had nothing to do that night because not enough people showed up for the dinner. This stunt is still used by many companies.

Our counsellor opened his attack with flattery. "You're young and could benefit most from this. We'd like to get you started on an investment program tonight." Getting started would cost only $105 — the down payment on an 80- by 125-foot homesite, just one lot removed from a boat canal (total price, $2,120 plus interest).

"We'd like to think about it," I said. "How about letting us have a brochure and a copy of the contract?" (Our counsellor had already started filling out a contract.)

"Now what could you possibly know in a day or two that you don't know right now? You can change your mind within six months — *six months* — and get every cent back. Where could you get a better offer than that?"

At another table a salesman leaped to his feet. "I want a hold on lot 33-C," he yelled.

Our man continued: "Do you realize you make $140 *immediately* when you sign this paper? We're giving a 2 percent bonus discount tonight, and there's a $100 deduction just for going down there."

When I hesitated, he exclaimed: "Remember, procrastination is the mother of disappointment."

I asked if he really believed that the lot he was trying to sell us was a good, sound, promising investment.

"Why, it's a *wonderful* investment."

"Will it be just as wonderful next week?"

"Uh, well . . . of course it will . . ."

"Fine! Just let us have that brochure and contract. I'd like our attorney to look at it."

"You sign that contract now and show it to your attorney tomorrow, and if he finds a single thing wrong with it, I guarantee you that we'll tear it up and send back your money."

Ginny interrupted. "We just had to pay our income tax, and we don't have $105 in the bank." That didn't bother him.

"We always hear that sort of thing from people," he snapped impatiently. He echoed the earlier question of the sales manager: "Do you realize that 92 percent of the people in America live beyond their incomes?"

Ginny said that she preferred not to live beyond ours.

Our man didn't give up, though. We were his last chance. At the other tables that were still occupied the counsellors seemed to be meeting with similar resistance. Voices were rising noticeably. A few feet away the sales manager was gesturing vigorously at a stubborn guest.

Finally we stood up and said that we were *not* signing anything that night. Our counsellor rose too, and with a deft motion he managed to position himself between us and the door. That maneuver led to ten more minutes of verbal bombardment. It was close to 10:30 P.M. When we still refused

to yield, he made an inconspicuous gesture and reinforcements
— three men — began arriving.

"What seems to be the difficulty?" asked one, smiling
graciously.

"Oh, nothing much, really," said our counsellor. "They say
they haven't got the cash."

"Is *that* all? Did you tell them that 92 percent of the people
in this country live beyond their incomes? You told them about
the money-back guarantee, of course? And the exchange
privilege . . ."

The record played on, it looked as though we would be
spending the night there. The sales manager joined us. It
was like dealing with the forward wall of the Green Bay Packers.

"Let's get out of here," whispered Ginny, tugging at my arm.
I was all set to try an end run when our counsellor, momentarily
off guard, turned to speak to someone. We were able to plunge
straight through the line.

As we hurried toward the exit, I looked back and caught a
glimpse of the five salesmen. They were waving a surprised
and reluctant farewell, their obvious disappointment almost
completely masked by determined smiles.

There was one parting shot: "Remember, procrastination is
the mother of disappointment!"

10

The Harder They Sell

It's usually true that the worse the product, the harder the sell.
— Statement by a congressional investigator

W HEN GAC Properties, Inc., was called on the carpet in Rhode Island and California and subsequently was castigated in a report by the Council of Better Business Bureaus, Inc. (as recounted in Chapter 2), the president of the subsidiary proposed that the federal government undertake the licensing of all sales personnel employed in the interstate land industry.*

"It is my firm conviction that the only sensible way in which the problem areas . . . can be eliminated is the federal licensing of all salesmen," declared Frank M. Steffens in a Florida speech. He argued that salespeople would be less likely to stretch the truth if they knew that Uncle Sam was keeping an eye on them, ready to revoke their licenses if they stepped out of line. GAC had made strenuous efforts to upgrade its sales force through better training, recruitment, and management, Steffens said,

---

*A bill to require federal licensing was subsequently introduced in congress by Senator Vance Hartke of Indiana.

but he added, "The bitter truth remains — we will never be able to completely assure that serious sales misrepresentations won't occur in the field." This, he asserted, "remains the industry's enigma, its most serious problem."

Steffens said in effect that his company and others in the multi-billion-dollar installment land industry are unable to control their sales personnel and that it will take nothing less than the U.S. government to do the job. Just why it is that land salesmen should be harder to restrain than, for example, an Avon products seller was not explained, but the inferences in Steffens's proposition are quite clear: most of the iniquities in land selling are committed by sales people; their employers are pure and good of heart.

Land-company executives have a conditioned reflex by which they blame salespeople for nearly everything wrong in the industry; thus it should be enlightening to know how some companies recruit and train their salespeople.

First let's run through a few excerpts from tape recordings furnished by GAC to its sales managers for their trainees. One tape begins with an anecdote. An 18-year-old farm boy asked for a job in a bank. The president asked if he had any banking experience. The answer was no. What education? Seventh grade. Well, why did he consider himself qualified for banking? The youth replied that he and his friends often staged a contest in which they hurled cow manure on the side of a barn. The thrower who could make it stick the longest was the winner. "And I usually win," said the job applicant. He was hired immediately.

The narrator of the tape then remarks: "Now, we've got a lot of guys around there who know how to throw it, but very few who know how to make it stick." He goes on to say:

"If there is nothing else you have learned in the sales profession, I think that the next few words are the most important in your whole career. Everyone has one thing in common — a hot button that affects us from the day we're born until the day we die. And that is the need for more money. Money is the buffer against all the adversities that can happen to you in your lifetime. That's why the millionaire is looking for his second million. That's why you and your prospect want to accumulate wealth. It's not greed — it's the cushion needed to battle disease, inflation, and taxes. It's the security blanket that every human being needs and strives for: the confidence and peace of mind needed to face the uncertain future.

"So basically, what are you saying to your prospect? 'Mr. Jones, we agree that we all have a need for more money. Now, GAC has a plan that will accomplish this for you. So you do this, Mr. Jones, and GAC will do this, and together we'll both prosper.' And that, believe it or not, is the key to every sale that has ever been made, or will be made, as long as human beings remain human."

The author and speaker of those lines was Harold Liberman, GAC's sales training director between December, 1968, and January, 1971. At this writing he is the sales training director at General Development Corporation.

On the tapes Liberman gives elaborate instructions for activating humanity's "hot button." Salespeople should start their pitches with "approach openers."

One is the *attention-getting approach:* "Mr. Jones, do you know that the Social Security Board [sic] in Washington, D.C., says that 85 percent of all people who reach the age of 65 have less than $250 to their name? We have a plan to get you out of that category."

If that fizzles, there is the *sincerity approach:* "Mrs. Jones, I want you to be more anxious to buy than I am to sell. . . . All I want to talk about is your future and your family's future."

When the prospect is reasonably alert, the salesman should "move quickly into the body of the presentation." The strategy here is to tell as little as possible. Liberman says, "We have a saying in sales training: know it all but don't say it all. Facts alone do not sell. Nobody buys nuts and bolts."

Then comes the moment of truth — the close. Liberman explained how to handle any situation that might arise at this crucial point. If the prospect seems skeptical, he should be sounded out with a *trial close.* Liberman said: "Trial closes are questions that are structured so that each answer is affirmative."

Example: "Mr. Jones, the potential benefits of our land savings plan will give security to you and your family. Don't you think they deserve it?"

The trial close can be followed with an *action close* ("You okay it here, and I'll okay it here, and we can get started."); a *question close* ("Where do you want us to send your plat map?"); the *choice close* ("Do you want a waterfront or nonwaterfront lot? Corner or inside? Do you want to pay five or ten percent down?"); or the *minor point close* ("Do you want your first name or initials on the agreement?").

"One of the greatest closes is also the shortest," Liberman told his trainees. "It goes like this: 'Mr. Jones, what would you do if you had $15,000?' When he answers, you say: 'Good. Let's get started.'"

The bane of all high-pressure salespeople is a prospect who wants time to think it over. "Prospects use that stall quite often because they've learned that it works," Liberman said. In an attempt to keep the ploy from working too often he offers an assortment of one-liners: "What will you know tomorrow that you don't know today?" "Every day you wait you pay more." "How can you lose with a company like ours?" "Every day you wait puts you 350 pieces of land away from your highest potential profit."

When a prospect capitulates, the salesperson should charge in with a spiel designed to head off any change of mind. "It is extremely important to make the buyer look better in his eyes and his loved one's eyes for having made a positive decision," Liberman stated. This is done by saying: "Mr. Jones, I want to congratulate you on taking the first step toward securing your family's future. They should be proud of you. There aren't many people left who think of their loved ones first."

There are always the people who get cold feet in the harsh light of day. For them there's the button-up. Liberman recommends this "typical button-up to handle an objection we all know well. It's called buyer's remorse." To apply it the salesperson says:

Mr. and Mrs. Jones, I want to congratulate you on your decision. But I also have a warning for you. Something is going to happen about 24 hours from now. You're going to look at each other and say: "Oh, my God, what did we do?" You've had that happen before, haven't you? Well, when it happens I want you to remember that you made two decisions. . . . First, you decided that this company operates in a legal manner — that we would, as we are required to do by law, return your money if you asked for it. You also decided that it is better to temporarily suspend your spending while you investigate our offer at no risk. It isn't going to cost you a single penny to find out if it's a good investment.

GAC officials say that the Liberman tapes are no longer used by the company, and Liberman insists that his new employer, General Development, does not employ such tactics. "The state of the art of the industry two or three years ago was this approach, you see," he told the author. "At that time money was not, or investment was not considered a taboo. You know we still talked about the fact that you might make money in real estate. At the present time that's looked upon with disfavor. Like styles, you know, things change."

The kind of gimmickry set forth in the Liberman tapes is common in the business. A manual used by salespeople for California City during N. K. Mendelsohn's reign there contained this bit of wisdom:

. . . 90 percent of the people buy because they lack the courage to continue saying no. Thus, in our sales presentation at one point or another, we are certainly going to use both persistence and persuasion, knowing that if we persuaded our customer to save his money and invest it in a parcel of land, we are doing him a favor, and that otherwise the money would probably be spent on some foolish and unessential thing.

A guidebook used by Horizon Corporation teaches something called the SATMC (pronounced "sat-mack") for handling excuses. Here's how the system works:

S — *Smile.* A smile is disarming and shows that we are not concerned about the excuse.

A — Agree. This removes any possibility of any argumentative attitude.

T — Turn the excuse. Show the other side of the question.

M — More value and reasons to buy. This is one reason why we skip many points during our sales talk. We have many new things to go back to and show if he brings up some excuse for not buying at the close of the presentation.

C — Close differently. Ask for the order by using a new "choice" question. If you have already asked for the order by saying, "Which of these properties do you like?," this time you might ask, "Would it be convenient to send these payments before the 15th (of the month) or after?" Or, "How do you usually take care of things like this — cash or pay a little each month?"

Horizon also tells its salespeople how to handle difficulties that might develop when both husband and wife are present for a sales pitch. If one speaks to the other, the salesperson should interrupt by saying: "Mr. and Mrs. Jones, I believe that's my question." The interruption is made, of course, to forestall any doubts, objections, or skepticism that might result from a huddle between the man and his wife and to keep them from doing too much thinking.

Silence is anything but golden for high-voltage salespeople. When it occurs, says the Horizon manual, the salesperson should interrupt by saying: "Well, Mrs. Jones, there is a slight charge for my visit here this evening (motion with your hand and smile) — half a glass of water." As she leaves the room, get Mr. Jones interested and agreeing with you, nodding, the manual adds.

In the event that an unconvinced Mrs. Jones is not checkmated by this ploy, the salesperson fires a question:

If you did decide to make the program part of your investment portfolio, Mr. Jones, could the pennies a day make you a candidate for the County Poorhouse? Mrs. Jones, would it take the mustard off the hot dogs or the syrup off the pancakes?

Of course not! So, you see, we're talking about *making* money, *not* spending it.

When a prospect protests that he or she simply can't afford to buy land, the salesperson is advised by Horizon to proceed as follows:

1. Smile.
2. Tell the prospect: "Mr. Jones, I understand just how you feel. Most men have felt the same way at first thought, and it is true that we cannot afford everything. But when it comes to investments, which mean so much to the future of your family, most men agree that this program is, after all, not an expense but an investment. On second thought, most men say, 'I guess it is not a case of can I afford it, but can I afford to be without it?' Here is a particular parcel that I am sure will interest you . . ."
3. Ask him to get started. Hand him the pen.

If that maneuver fails, the salesperson should:

1. Smile.
2. Tell the prospect: "Mr. Jones, we don't question for one minute that you have a place for your money. But it is the most natural thing in the world to put things off, although the longer you do the harder it becomes to decide. Six months from today can become a tremendous obstacle in the future. The sooner that you make an investment like this, the more you will get out of it, isn't that true? The study of the lives of great men who have made their fortunes in real estate have always fascinated me."
3. Ask him to get started. Hand him the pen.

In an 18-page sales memo James O. Foote, president of Chase Continental Corporation, outlines 9 sure-fire closing techniques, including the *sharp angle close:*

Of course we use sharp angles. You're a sucker if you don't. When you use this close, you wait until [the prospect] asks something such as: "Could we leave our boat at the dock?" You guys make the mistake of saying yes. What you should say is: "Do you want the lot if you can use the dock?" You've got a sale when he says yes. You have turned the question into a sharp angle close.

Then there's the *be back close:*

We don't talk much about the *be back close* because we don't believe in it. We believe and teach the *one shot close* — but if you do not close on the first shot and call on the prospect at his home, *please* do not go in and say: "Did you think it over?" If you do, you're dead! When you call back, start your conversation by saying: "I'm sorry, sir, but I forgot to tell you . . ." Then tell him something new — and go through the whole story again.

In executing the *one shot close,* nailing down a sale right after making the original pitch, salespeople should do as follows, says Foote:

Do not use the word "contract." Use the word "agreement." And don't ask the prospect if he wants the lot. Ask him a question and write the answer on your agreement. Ask, "What is your correct name, sir? What is your correct mailing address?" And so on through the agreement. Remember, if he has let you fill out the agreement, *he has bought.* You assume he has bought. Okay, what do you do when you get to the bottom? Don't ask him to sign. You know what's wrong with the word "sign." You have been taught all your life to read every word, be careful, beware, don't sign anything. So you ask him to *okay* the agreement. He won't sign it but he *will* okay it. Strange but true.

If for some reason the prospect doesn't okay the "agreement," there is always the *lost sale close.* Foote describes it:

This is the close to use when everything else has failed. This is how it works: Get ready to get out of your car as if it's all over. Put on a sad, serious face, and say:

"Before you go, let me apologize for being so inept a salesman. I must be inept because I did not make you feel the way I do about [the development]. If I had made you feel the way I do, you would now own a lot here and you, sir, could have enjoyed some of the best fishing in the state. Your wife could have gotten away from the crowded, noisy city, and your children would be able to take advantage of the open air, the swimming, water skiing, and fishing.

"And I want you to know I am truly sorry. As you can see, I make my living this way. So that I don't make the same mistake again, would you mind telling me what I did that was wrong?"

They will. They don't want to hurt you. And when they mention some objection, you come back and say: "Golly, didn't I tell you about that?" And you're back in the running for a try at another close.

The toughest close to learn — but the most important to know — is the *final objection close*. Foote says:

> Normally when you reach for your first close, a man seldom says no; he gives you an objection. You answer the objection. Does this get you a close? Hell, no! All it does is pop another question. So you get in a contest. As fast as you kill one objection, he pops up with another.

Of course, everybody who sells land does not engage in this sort of hard-sell approach. The occupation embraces some sincere and reputable people, but unfortunately their number appears to be relatively small.

Although many land sellers give themselves impressive titles such as "land counsellor," "investment counsellor," or "land-investment specialist," practically none of them are qualified as investment advisers or financial planners. Unlike stockbrokers they are not under orders from their industry's hierarchy to warn customers that they should use only surplus funds for investment.

Many installment land hawkers know little if anything about real estate, let alone investing. In some situations a salesperson does not need even a real estate license. This is true of personnel who host dinner parties at which sales are not consummated. In Pennsylvania, where land company officials are not required to have licenses, some outfits make all their salesmen "vice presidents."

The land-selling gentry includes former carnival barkers, car-wash attendants, bus drivers, press agents, wrestlers, bouncers, and hawkers of everything from deodorants to vacuum cleaners to worthless securities. Many people with other full-time occupations sell land in the evenings and on weekends, and some college students help to meet expenses by selling part time. A classified advertisement of Horizon Corporation tells something of the type of personnel that are sought:

Salesmen . . . HORIZON WANTS YOU NOW. Earn $30,000 annually with a $50-million national corporation. HOME IMPROVEMENTS, BOOKS, VACUUM CLEANERS, LAND INSURANCE, SECURITIES, ETC. . . . For the man that wants to make money and move up.

Before this chapter comes to a sharp angle close, let us consider Frank Steffens's suggestion for federal licensing of salespeople. It is doubtful that such licensing would help the public, but it would probably aid the salespeople. Flashing a federal permit might be more effective and impressive than a sledgehammer close.

"Persistent misrepresentation by salesmen demands an approving or permissive attitude at the top," wrote Kenneth Slocum, the *Wall Street Journal* reporter who broke the story of the scathing investigative report about Gulf American Corporation in 1967. The head of another major land development company observed: "There is no such thing as bad salesmen and good management in one company." It will take much more than surveillance of salesmen to clean up the industry. As long as companies are permitted to subdivide land without regard for need and to exaggerate the investment value of lots, such problems will continue.

If Steffens and his colleagues sincerely want to keep their troops in line, there are a few simple things they could do: they could see that all prospective buyers get meaningful disclosure; they could order a halt to the strong-arming of prospects at dinner parties; and they could insist that salespeople tell the truth about the value of unimproved lots as speculative investments.

If they did all that, however, GAC and most other companies might find themselves out of the land sales business.

11

The Failure of Government Regulation

I$_F$ land subdividers were compelled to observe the kinds of rules that govern most other providers of goods and services, many of them would have to change their ways drastically or go out of business.

The consumer movement that commenced in the mid-1960s wrought sweeping changes in the American marketplace. Cigarette packages must display health-hazard warnings as well as tar and nicotine contents; drugs must prove their effectiveness; automobiles must meet more rigid safety standards; advertisers must substantiate their claims to the satisfaction of the Federal Trade Commission (FTC); and credit merchants must disclose loan charges in plain English.

Spurred by the rising tide of consumerism and environmental concern, the federal government has cracked down on deceptive advertising, shoddy merchandise, unsafe products, worthless drugs, misleading labels, and unfair practices. The Campbell Soup Company was ordered to stop using marbles to accentuate the solid contents of vegetable soup shown on the screen. The ITT-Continental Baking Company not only was directed to stop implying that Profile Bread could cause weight reduction but was compelled to confess in subsequent ads that claims to that effect had been exaggerated. Other such examples abound.

In contrast, for the most part the consumer revolution has not caught up with installment land companies. Swampland, desert wastes, and other real estate of dubious value are still sold as "investments" to people of modest means. Despite a federal "disclosure" law, many land hustlers still conceal vital information or fail to explain it adequately.

There are many contributing factors to the failure of land sales companies to reveal all the facts. For one thing, not enough people in positions of influence are aware of the problem and its consequences. This is true also of many who are victimized.

"There isn't much public outcry because defrauded buyers usually don't realize what has happened to them," says Winton D. Woods, Jr., professor of law at the University of Arizona. "If you buy a piece of carpet that falls apart in three months, you're really going to howl. But if you pay $35 a month for a piece of land you don't see and won't use for 15 years, you won't know you've been had for some time."

The myth persists that almost any piece of land, no matter how unpromising, will eventually reward its owner, as does the notion that anybody who gets rooked in a land deal has only himself or herself to blame. Land frauds, while extensive, do not threaten to rupture the nation's economic fabric, as did the debauchery that preceded the 1929 stock market crash and the subsequent Depression, which eventually led to federal regulation of the securities industry.

In the main, however, land frauds continue because elements of the land industry have succeeded in fending off meaningful regulations at the federal level and in some states, by lobbying, issuing propaganda, and making political deals. Installment land selling is immensely lucrative, and the sellers intend to keep it that way. Some salespeople have not hesitated to bribe or threaten public officials, to malign critics, or to intimidate the news media. (A developer in California dealt quite effectively with a newspaper that had relentlessly attacked him. He bought it.)

The need for reforms has been recognized for decades by consumer advocates, responsible public officials, and some newspeople. In the early 1950s a *Miami Herald* reporter named Steve Trumbull, who had previously reported about crime in Al Capone's Chicago, revealed in a lengthy series of articles that the selling of underwater "homesites" in Florida had again become a racket of massive proportions. The Florida legislature met in an emergency session in 1956 and rushed through a bill that provided $100,000 fines and up to five years imprisonment for anyone convicted of publishing false or misleading information about real estate offerings. That measure was a monumental flop because it simply was not enforced. Spurred by still more Trumbull revelations, the legislature passed a law, in 1959, which empowered the Florida Real Estate Commission to review and censor the advertising of companies selling Florida land to residents of other states.

By 1959 the spectacular successes of the Florida promoters were attracting imitators, and shady subdivision had begun to proliferate elsewhere — so much so that the National Better Business Bureau, Inc. (NBBB), issued a declaration that land swindles in Florida and the Southwest threatened to become a national scandal.

Farris Bryant, then the governor of Florida, bristled with indignation and demanded that the NBBB name names. To have done so, of course, would have left the association wide open to damage suits, and it wisely demurred. However, some Florida newspapers with heavy libel insurance undertook investigations of their own. The evidence that the reporters turned up made it plain that the NBBB charges were, if anything, understated. One offering that had been cleared by the Real Estate Commission, for example, was Florida Ranchette Acres, a four-square-mile chunk of watery boondocks near Daytona Beach that, for purposes of illustrating brochures, had been decorated with a model home — or "ranchette" — at its entrance.

"Own a valuable tract on the edge of Florida's boom area," said the brochure. "Secure your future — *now!* Florida Ranchettes offer an opportunity for people of modest means to invest in Florida's future by purchasing a sizable tract of tropical beauty. . . . Not a wilderness, but a beautiful . . . garden spot . . . high, dry land." In reality, much of the land is under water, a fact that was brought to light by the *Daytona Beach News-Journal.*

It quickly became clear that something had to be done; the governor's credibility and the state's integrity were being jeopardized. Governor Bryant appointed an investigating committee, which was composed mostly of developers, realty brokers, and lawyers, and announced: "National publicity has been focused recently on the sale of subdivided land, and Florida has drawn the least adverse publicity of any state. However, I would like to see Florida remain in the forefront in its efforts to protect the ultimate purchaser of Florida land."

Several of the people on Bryant's committee were openly hostile to the idea of saddling subdividers with stricter regulations. Morton Rothenberg, an attorney who represents several swamp sellers and who himself heads at least four corporations that sell submarginal land, said: "You can't hold people's hands when they sign a contract [a favorite expression of land hustlers]." But testimony taken at a series of hearings held in the state of Florida by the Bryant committee left no doubt that land sales bamboozlement was indeed present on a grand scale.

The committee recommended enactment of a more comprehensive law and the creation of a new board to administer it — the Florida Installment Land Sales Board (FILSB). The legislature did so later that same year. The committee also recommended the formation by the installment land industry of a "self-policing" organization, and the industry happily obliged. It established the Installment Land Sales and Development Association of Florida, Inc. (ILSDAF). ILSDAF had its headquarters one floor above the FILSB's offices, in Tampa.

ILSDAF's chief purpose, according to its widely publicized "code of ethics," was "to establish and maintain standards of ethical conduct and methods of operation" and to make "full disclosure" to land buyers. Members were entitled to display, in their sales material and elsewhere, an imposing "seal of approval" bearing the words: "ETHICS . . . INTEGRITY . . . PROTECTION."

ILSDAF's members included Dory Auerbach, who was later convicted of mail fraud; Gulf American Corporation, which in 1967 pleaded guilty to the charge of unethical selling practices; Sam Sacks, who was convicted of mail fraud in 1969*; and All-State Development Corporation, several officers of which were indicted on 30 counts of mail fraud in connection with sales at Rocket City, a promotion in central Florida that went down in flames in the early 1960's, leaving more than 2,000 lot buyers holding the bag. Other ILSDAF members included Florida Ranchettes, Inc., and Firstamerica Development Corporation. The organization's secretary and general counsel was Morton Rothenberg. A few years later, when ILSDAF changed its name to Florida Land Association, Fuller Warren became its president. It is hardly surprising then, that ILSDAF was seen to do little to protect the public interest.

Other attempts at "self-policing" were also colossal failures. In 1963 the NBBB sponsored a meeting of representatives of the land sales industry in Scottsdale, Arizona, to propose a ten-point program of self-regulation, but the program was never put into effect.

Florida's alacrity in pushing for legislative reforms — or appearing to do so — was provoked in part by the fear that the federal government might one day preempt the field of land sales regulation. Indeed, Congress had already shown concern over reports that millions of Americans were being defrauded.

Because so many of the victims of land sales were people of retirement age and older, the Senate's Special Committee on Aging began making inquiries, in 1963. An awkward situation occurred because the committee's chairman was George Smath-

---

*Sacks appealed, and his case was dismissed.

ers, then a Florida senator. "I don't think land frauds are a problem in my state," Smathers pointedly asserted in a preliminary discussion concerning matters of procedure.

"Well, swamp merchants in Florida have relieved a good many old folks of their savings," rejoined another committee member.

Despite Smather's antipathy a special investigative unit was formed, a subcommittee on frauds and misrepresentations affecting the elderly. Senator Harrison A. Williams, Jr., a liberal Democrat from New Jersey, was named chairman. He scheduled three days of hearings in June, 1964. As a news editor of the *Daytona Beach News-Journal* and a contributor to *Florida Trend* magazine, I had written a number of articles about land sales; consequently the subcommittee asked me to organize a panel of witnesses to discuss the situation.

Warren Greenwood, a real estate broker and appraiser, and Robert Doyle, planning director for the East-Central Florida Regional Planning Council, agreed to appear with me. Greenwood and I testified about several swampy subdivisions near Daytona Beach, including University Highlands, the Firstamerica Development Corporation offering discussed in Chapter 7. We displayed sales materials for the various properties, compared them to photographs of the land itself, and submitted signed statements and other data from engineers, geologists, and public officials attesting to the condition of the properties. Doyle talked about the difficulties that such subdivisions create for planners, builders, and government officials.

Appearing next were the Installment Land Sales Board's chairman, Marshall M. Criser, and its executive director, John W. McWhirter. They told the subcommittee that a few problems did indeed exist but that they would be solved in short order. "We feel that we should be given the opportunity to prove that the [board] can do the job it was created to do," Criser said.

Senator Smathers, who was not present while Greenwood, Doyle, and I were giving our presentations, entered the hearing room just as McWhirter wound up his testimony. He questioned McWhirter about the existing land sales laws:

SMATHERS: As I understand our problem, we have had in the past some difficulty, but the state legislature, did it not, pass a law and set up a committee?

MC WHIRTER: Yes, sir. That is correct.

SMATHERS: It has been my opinion that while we had a great deal of this in years gone by, comparatively speaking, there is no longer a great abuse of this selling business, that is, selling through the mail and defrauding elderly people through the mail. Am I wrong or right about that, Mr. McWhirter?

MC WHIRTER: It has modified to a great degree.

SMATHERS: Under that new law which was passed . . . do you have the authority to stop that type of advertising when your board thinks it is misleading?

MC WHIRTER: Very definitely. Yes, sir.

SMATHERS: All of this is actually for the protection of the people who do come to Florida and who do wish to buy lots, singular [sic] or more, and spend the remaining part of their life living in Florida?

MC WHIRTER: That is correct. Yes, sir.

SMATHERS: Do you think that even the evil at present going on, that your particular group will be able to at least minimize that which now exists?

MC WHIRTER: Yes, sir. I do not think we can stamp it out. I do not think we will ever stamp it out.

SMATHERS: Because you think it is a human problem of overselling?

MC WHIRTER: Yes, sir.

SMATHERS: We must stop any company that has a pattern of this kind of thing. It is not fair to the other good developers, and you know that most of the developers in our state are a credit to the business. Is that not correct?

MC WHIRTER: Yes, sir.

The interrogation left no doubt about the senator's position, and no one who knew him was surprised. As Robert Sherrill notes in his brilliant *Gothic Politics in the Deep South:* "Senator Smathers has always been keen for land promotions in Florida."

As he left the hearing room, Smathers was asked by news reporters what he thought about proposals for empowering the federal government to police interstate land sales. "I don't think there should be further federal regulation of this any more than there should be federal regulation of the auto-building

industry," he replied. (One year later an obscure lawyer named
Ralph Nader unleashed history's largest consumer movement
by exposing serious safety defects in a number of automotive
products. Today the government tells the automobile industry
quite a bit about how to build cars.)

ILSDAF had been invited to send representatives to testify at
the subcommittee hearings, but it politely declined. A Firstamerica lawyer who was present, C. Aubrey Vincent of Daytona
Beach, did not challenge any statements made about that company. But when reports of the testimony reached Fuller Warren,
Firstamerica vice-president and former Florida governor, Warren dashed off a statement, copies of which were dispatched to
the subcommittee and to every major newspaper in Florida.
Excerpts follow:

> First, Paulson is a pliant hireling of a vicious and untruthful
> so-called newspaper in Daytona Beach, which is owned and profit-
> ably exploited by two fanatical eccentrics.* This organ of intoler-
> ance disguised as a newspaper fought me viciously and unfairly
> in my 1948 campaign for Governor, and during my four-year
> service as Governor, this vicious medium of misinformation
> published recurring false allegations about me and my adminis-
> tration. . . .
> Second, Paulson's testimony is a misleading and deceitful bag
> of half-truths and half-lies. Paulson deceitfully attempted to con-
> vey the false impression that University Highlands . . . is mainly
> swampland. He testified under oath that University Highlands in-
> cludes "more than 12,000 acres." This testimony is not true. It is
> comprised of 9,420 acres. Next, Paulson's testimony that Univer-
> sity Highlands is mainly swampland is not true. The minimum
> elevation above sea level of this land is 31 feet. . . . I have personal-
> ly driven over University Highlands in an automobile, and I
> have flown over University Highlands in an airplane, and I
> state categorically that it is not mainly swampland. . . .
> One Warren L. Greenwood also gave misleading and inaccu-

---

* I appeared at the hearings as an individual, not as a representative of
the newspaper or as anyone's "pliant hireling." To this day nobody has dis-
puted our testimony except Warren, who submitted nothing to substantiate
his outburst.

rate testimony about University Highlands. . . . Greenwood has a cheek-by-jowl relationship with the so-called newspaper that was behind Paulson's misleading and deceitful testimony. Greenwood was this so-called newspaper's pet candidate for tax assessor of Volusia County in the 1964 Democratic primary. This power-hungry newspaper attempted to foist Greenwood upon the people of Volusia County in order to put into effect a vicious system of property assessment. . . . Despite this so-called newspaper's frantic efforts, Greenwood was humiliatingly defeated by a vote of about 2 to 1. So, he was speaking as a defeated, disgruntled, and rejected candidate when he poured out before a Senate subcommittee a mass of misleading and deceitful testimony about University Highlands. . . .*

A few days after Greenwood and I returned to Florida, the Daytona Beach Board of Realtors (of which Greenwood was a former president) entertained a motion to censure us for having made statements in Washington that might reflect unfavorably against Florida real estate. The board, like others of its kind throughout the country, is an affiliate of the National Associ-ation of Real Estate Boards (NAREB), which is forever pro-claiming from the rooftops that its members subscribe to a code of ethics and therefore are to be trusted. The censure resolution probably resulted from testimony we gave about Canaveral Lake Estates, a swampy investment-acreage offering that had been conceived and executed by a prominent member of the Daytona board. His partners in the scheme included a prominent local banker, the president of a local manufacturing company, and several other civic leaders of supposedly good reputation. We did not name these people at the hearings because it was pos-sible that they did not realize that the offering was a flim-flam; they could have been duped into buying shares by the realtor. In any event, the censure motion was defeated. Soon afterward records in the county courthouse indicated that the local people had liquidated their interest in Canaveral Lake Estates.

During the next several years Florida got its chance to en-

---

* Greenwood ran again for tax assessor in 1968 and was elected.

force its new law. The Senate subcommittee concluded that federal controls were urgently needed and made a strong recommendation to that effect. It was not until 1966, however, that the necessary legislation was introduced. In the meantime it became increasingly clear that things weren't going well with Florida's new regulatory régime. The committee that had been commissioned by Governor Bryant to investigate land selling abuses had proposed that the new Installment Land Sales Board consist of three members representing the public and two representing the installment land industry. But the land companies, applying their formidable lobbying muscle, persuaded the legislature to reverse that order, and the industry gained control of the agency. The foxes were guarding the chickens.*

Unfortunately the new law contained a gaping loophole through which a number of land sellers escaped the board's jurisdiction altogether — by conveying deeds to lot buyers at the time of sale and taking *mortgages* instead of installment contracts. The law covered only *installment* sales.

The new law provided for "full disclosure" through property reports, and thousands of buyers complained because they failed to get them. Haydon Burns, who succeeded Bryant as governor of Florida, stacked the new board with developers and their friends. At one point the membership included Leonard Rosen, chairman of the Gulf American Corporation, and three men who did business with the company. The board received more complaints about Gulf American than about any other company in the state, but little was done to rectify them. Gulf American had already become something of a household word in the lexicon of land sales legerdemain.

In Washington in 1966 Senator Williams introduced a bill providing for federal control of land sales, which was adopted in 1968 as the Interstate Land Sales Full Disclosure Act. Leon-

---

*One of the developer members was Gerald Gould, president of Lehigh Acres Development, Inc., developer of Lehigh Acres. In 1969 Lehigh Acres Development, Inc., was charged by the New York attorney general's office with selling property in the state without authorization and making misleading offers of vacation trips. The company was fined $2,000, and it agreed in a consent order to discontinue the violations.

ard Rosen was among the witnesses asked to testify about Florida conditions before a Senate banking subcommittee. He ducked several invitations, contending that the "pressure of business" made it impossible for him to get to Washington, though Senator Williams caustically noted that Gulf American had an office in Baltimore, 40 miles away from Washington and that "the trains are running."

Rosen's evasiveness was too much for even free-wheeling Florida to endure; Rosen quietly resigned from the board. Even so, in 1967 a grand jury in Collier County, a center of swamp selling, urged that the land board be replaced or realigned to diminish the influence of developers. "The grand jury is of the unanimous opinion that the effectiveness of the FILSB leaves much to be desired," the panel said.

Florida faced a choice of acting against flim-flams — at least to a degree — or losing its regulatory function to Washington by default. The latter was unthinkable. To head off such a disaster the legislature abolished the Installment Land Sales Board and created a new commission, called the Florida Land Sales Board (FLSB).* The FLSB had seven members, only two of whom were developers (a good case could be made for the proposition that such an agency should have *no* developers).

It was about this time that the Gulf American affair discussed in Chapter 2 broke into the open. Obviously the board had to do *something* about Gulf; how else could Florida convince Washington that errant subdividers henceforth would be dealt with severely?

Such assurances would have been ludicrous had Gulf been permitted to carry on as before. While the penalties against the company were anything but severe, the land board's stiffened posture looked impressive at the time. In December, 1967, Carl A. Bertoch, who had succeeded McWhirter as executive director, told Associated Press that the era of "shenanigans and hanky-panky" in Florida land sales had ended. "This new board

---

* ILSDAF, the "self-policing" industry group, immediately changed its name to Florida Land Association. The association later named Fuller Warren as its president.

is saying that Florida land can be purchased by the public with confidence," said Bertoch. Florida authorities finally persuaded Washington to allow them to continue handling the regulatory job themselves. The activities that were described in Chapter 7 should give the reader some idea of how well they performed.

In 1970 the state again replaced its regulatory apparatus. As part of a sweeping governmental reorganization the legislature placed a number of regulatory functions under a totally new agency, the Department of Business Regulation. The Florida Land Sales Board was abolished, and its operations were transferred to a unit of the new department called the Division of Florida Land Sales. There is no longer any policy-making board for land sales as such; the division is run by a gubernatorial appointee named A.L. Baker, who came to the job from private industry with no previous connection with land selling or business regulation. Baker and a staff of 25, operating on an annual budget of under $250,000, are responsible for keeping more than 350 subdividers in line. How well they succeed remains to be seen. "It's all we can do just to try and keep our heads above water," Baker told the author soon after taking over.

Between 1969 and 1972 the number of states having some form of land-sales controls jumped from 20 to 35, but the laws tended to be weakest in states where land hustlers are most active, such as Florida. State laws are notable for their lack of uniformity. Eight states classify out-of-state subdivision offerings as securities — California, Georgia, Kansas, Maine, Minnesota, Missouri, Tennessee, Vermont, and West Virginia. Those states take the admirable position that subdivision offerings sold as speculative investments should be regulated like sales of stocks, bonds, and other securities because they resemble security offerings and many people invest their savings in them. In some states land salespeople must be licensed as securities salespeople.

New York state is not among these eight, but it does have a realistic regulatory program, adopted soon after *Newsday,* in a superb series of exposés by Robert Caro, revealed that thousands of New York residents were being fleeced by crooked subdividers. New York not only requires exhaustively detailed disclosure by subdividers who sell to New York citizens, but it prohibits the sale of land deemed worthless or unusable. Subdividers who promise to improve the land they sell must post performance bonds. Every subdivision offering is personally inspected by agents of New York's Department of State. Many offerings with routine clearance from federal authorities have been banned in New York. Since April, 1969, when the federal law became operative, the office of New York Attorney General Louis J. Lefkowitz has obtained close to $7 million in restitution for victimized land buyers.

The law that comes closest to being a model is the one applied by California to out-of-state subdivisions. Significantly, many of the largest land companies, including GAC Corporation and Horizon Corporation, have not met California's requirements and are not permitted to sell there. From September, 1963, until the time this book went to press, the state did not authorize sales in California of *any* subdivided land located in Florida. Besides treating lots as securities, California applies what is called the "fair, just, and equitable" test to subdivision offerings. Subdivisions are inspected and appraised, and if they are deemed unfair or too costly, the subdividers are denied permits to sell in California. Developers who promise improvements must put up financial security to guarantee them — usually a performance bond backed by a construction contract. In most cases the state requires developers to provide utilities within 18 months. "The longest we've *ever* let anybody go without putting in improvements is four years," says Hoyt Duty, senior legal counsel for the California Department of Real Estate.

California will not permit lots to be represented as speculative investments unless the subdivider submits an economic feasibility report containing "facts sufficient to justify" claims of investment value. "This investment value would also be verified by our experts before we would allow the property to be sold for such purposes," Duty asserts. "Any advertising extolling an investment value not supported by the report would be considered false and misleading and would justify this department in revoking the permit." Out-of-state lots may not be sold in California at a price above the value established by the Department of Real Estate.

In addition to these regulations the state forces subdividers to make full disclosure in extremely detailed public reports. Unfortunately California applies a different, less stringent set of rules to in-state subdivisions, which accounts in part for the difficulties the state has had with fast-buck subdivisions in California.

The federal government's track record in land sales regulation has been little better than Florida's in many ways. While the Williams law unquestionably has helped to wipe out many of the most nefarious schemes, it has also given an aura of respectability to subtler deceptions. The law can never erase all problems even if strictly interpreted and enforced to the letter. It is merely a disclosure statute, nothing else, and disclosure, while essential, is not sufficient by itself. Among other things, developers should be forced to guarantee improvements by putting up financial security such as bonds, and unfair offerings should be prohibited. But the Williams law could have accomplished a great deal. As originally drafted, the legislation would have been administered by the Securities and Exchange Commission (SEC).

The SEC was the logical agency to handle the assignment because of its long experience in administering the securities laws and its tough-minded attitude toward disclosure. Moreover, the SEC was ready and willing to take on the new duties. Its chairman at that time, Manuel F. Cohen, testified before a Senate banking subcommittee in 1966 that the land sales legislation "basically follows the pattern of the Securities Act of 1933, which is generally recognized to have dealt successfully with the problem at which it was aimed. We believe that the same technique could successfully be used in the regulation of the interstate sale of subdivision lots." Cohen mentioned also that many boiler-room securities salespeople who had been put out of business by the SEC "immediately moved to Miami and started boiler-room operations in unimproved real estate." Senator Walter F. Mondale (D-Minn.) opined that SEC-type disclosure would put a great many unsavory land promoters out of business as well. "It might well do that," Cohen replied.

Nobody knew this better than the promoters. For them SEC supervision could have been catastrophic. To fight it they mustered every available resource — all the more necessary when, in 1967, the Williams bill gained crucial momentum, thanks to President Lyndon B. Johnson, who reminded Congress in a special consumer message that many elderly persons had been swindled by land hustlers. "They have wasted much of their life savings on a useless piece of desert or swampland," he said. "Only the federal government can have effective authority over interstate mail-order sales."

Opposition to attempted legislation continued to grow. A bitter behind-the-scenes fight broke out in Congress. The interstate land dealers recruited an important ally, the National Association of Home Builders (NAHB), which considered federal regulation a deterrent to the burgeoning second-home market. Leon N. Weiner, then president of the NAHB, branded the bill's registration requirements as "elaborate, time-consuming, and expensive." He said that the legislation "needlessly imposes a heavy and expensive burden on our industry and on prospective home buyers." (This, of course, was false; if anything, the bill would have saved money for home buyers by minimizing the destruction and wasteful use of land resources.) The opponents to the bill put up such a squawk that backers of the measure were forced into a compromise under which responsibility for administering the regulatory program was assigned to the U.S. Department of Housing and Urban Development (HUD) rather than to the SEC. The *Congressional Quarterly* termed the change a "major victory" for the NAHB.

As finally enacted in 1968, the land-sales act provided that:
1. Anyone selling 50 or more unimproved lots — that is, lots

without buildings — in interstate commerce must register the subdivisions with HUD.

2. Prior to a sale, such sellers must give prospective customers a written property report setting forth about 19 items of information about the condition of the land offered and the terms of sale. The report must list distances between the subdivision and nearby communities; liens on the property; recreation facilities; availability of sewer and water service or of septic tanks and wells; information about present and proposed utility services and charges; the number of occupied homes in the development; the type of title the buyers will receive; soil and foundation conditions that could cause problems in construction or the use of septic tanks; and the estimated cost of drainage or special foundation or subsurface improvements that would be necessary for construction of buildings on the land.

3. Buyers who fail to receive a property report before signing a contract may cancel the agreement and get a refund. (The law was subsequently amended so that purchasers who inspect the property in person and certify in writing that they have done so relinquish this privilege.)

In addition to those provisions, the law empowered HUD to sue for injunctions to halt violations, and it provided for fines of up to $5,000 and five years' imprisonment for violators, who are also subject to civil liabilities. To administer the program HUD organized a division called the Office of Interstate Land Sales Registration (OILSR). The law and OILSR became operative in April, 1969. In February, 1970, OILSR issued a news release that said, in part: "Americans are buying more lots in land subdivisions today with greater confidence under a consumer-protection law" governing land sales. The OILSR's first administrator, Alfred J. Lehtonen, was quoted in the release as saying: "Our program is administered pretty much the way the Securities and Exchange Commission regulates securities offerings. We have a full-disclosure law. Buyers can decide to buy or not to buy on the basis of knowing exactly what they are offered." The buyer, added Lehtonen, was now "on an equal footing with the seller."

The release was widely quoted, and many subdividers began

proclaiming in advertisements and sales spiels that their offerings were registered with the government. Some salespeople went a step further and said — or implied — that registration constituted a government endorsement of the offering.

Was the new law really protecting buyers? In one of several attempts to find out I paid a call on OILSR in October, 1971, posing as a relative of some worried lot buyers. The card of the man who ushered me into his office identified him as Robert S. Thompson, director of the OILSR's examination division. His previous employer had been the Florida Land Sales Board. On a wall of his office was a handsome plaque on which that agency cited him for "outstanding service" in 1968 and 1969.

Using an assumed name, I told him that some out-of-town relatives had signed up to buy a lot in Charnita, a Pennsylvania recreational development (discussed in Chapter 5). I had chosen Charnita because of the development's pending difficulties with various official agencies and because I knew from a personal visit there that Charnita salespeople — or at least the ones I talked to — were specialists in high pressure.

Thompson removed his glasses and rubbed his eyes. "Well, I can make an appointment for you to look at the files. Would next week be all right?"

"No, I need the information now. These people are pretty upset."

"I see. Well, let me say this. Our director has checked out Charnita several times. I've checked it out myself several times. It's probably the most checked-out development we've got. And frankly, we think it's great!"

I told him that my cousins in Richmond would certainly be relieved to hear that. "But why was so much checking necessary?"

"Well, frankly, a few people have been giving the developers a hard time. I really think they've been harassed. They've made full disclosure, and that's all they're required to do."

But could I see the investigative file? Or a property report? Yes, but I'd have to have an appointment, and I'd have to pay $5 an hour for Xeroxing copies of the file plus $2.50 for a property report.

"You mean," I asked incredulously, "that a person who needs

information from this agency not only has to pay for it but has to wait several days to get it? Even when thousands of dollars are at stake?"

Thompson looked slightly uncomfortable. He protested that the OILSR simply didn't have the manpower to churn out copies of documents for everybody who walked in the door. But as a special favor for me he'd dig out the files. "You won't understand them, of course," he mumbled as he left the room.

Thompson returned with a foot-thick sheaf of papers. The property reports consisted of three long pages of fine print and were heavily sprinkled with terms such as "liens of judgment," "successors and assigns," and "easements for utilities." Interpreting the whole file would take considerable study — and possibly a lawyer or two — but a casual reading disclosed that (1) Charnita was heavily mortgaged; (2) if the mortgage holders foreclosed or if the developer went bankrupt, lot buyers who had not paid off their contracts would lose their equity; and (3) the Pennsylvania Department of Health had refused to issue building permits for large sections of the development because the soil had been deemed unsuitable for septic tanks.

The statements that really astonished me appeared in the last paragraph of the last page of the property report:

> Summary of pending litigation against Charnita, Inc.: An Equity Action was brought in the Adams County, Pennsylvania, Court by Tri-Township Citizens Association to require compliance with laws and regulations concerning land development. An appeal from the approval by the Liberty Township Supervisors of plats for Sections W, WA, RI, AD and AE has been filed in the same court by the Tri-Township Citizens Association. Class Suits have been filed by lot owners in Federal Court in the Middle District of Pennsylvania, alleging misrepresentation on the part of the Developer. A suit has been filed before the Federal Trade Commission alleging violations of the Federal "Truth in Lending Act." No final disposition has been made of any of these suits.

Thompson grimaced as I read the words. "Your reaction is to be expected, I suppose," he said. "Of course, this shows just how far we go in making them tell it like it is. But I'm not at all sure that it's fair to make them [the developers] include the statements about the suits. After all, those cases haven't been settled. Those people haven't been convicted of anything."

Neither was Jay Gould. Telling him that my cousins might want to know about the building bans, if not about the accusations, I requested a copy of the report. Thompson offered to mail them one — for $2.50. "But those people have just 24 hours to decide whether to go through with the deal," I said, telling another barefaced lie. Thompson finally agreed to sell me a copy.

Later I talked with Mrs. Gerald Perman of Chevy Chase, Maryland, a Pennsylvania property owner who has been active in the long and bitter fight against Charnita. She and others informed me that the adverse information in the property reports was added only because the Tri-Township Citizens Association, which spearheaded the fight (see Chapter 5), demanded repeatedly that it be put in the reports in the interests of consumer protection. OILSR resisted at first, and the association was compelled to apply pressure over a period of months, she said. "You would think you were dealing with lobbyists for the land sales industry," she asserted. "They gave us an incredible run-around. It was just unbelievable."

Convinced that some OILSR people were more interested in protecting subdividers than in protecting consumers, the Tri-Township Association had members pose as buyers and ask for information about various developments. Several of the members later swore in affidavits that OILSR personnel actually recommended the property they inquired about. The federal law specifically forbids any endorsements by government personnel.

An investigation by consumer-protection officials in Pennsylvania later revealed that the property reports still omitted important information, including the fact that on October 1, 1971, the state's Department of Environmental Resources imposed a ban on the construction of any buildings in Charnita except in cases where percolation tests showed that a lot was suitable for on-site sewage disposal equipment. State geological engineers had found previously that 85 percent of the ground was unsuitable for such installations. Holding tanks — containers emptied by collection trucks — were prohibited.

Also missing from the property reports was the fact that if the developer were to install a central sewerage system, which would cost an estimated $7 million, lot owners would be assessed $1,000 each per 100 feet of frontage and would have to pay $150 to $250 a year for using the facility. Nor did the reports mention that property owners were to be charged for paving roads in the development — a project that also could cost millions.

In November, 1971, the consumer-protection bureau of the Pennsylvania attorney-general's office dispatched an 11-page letter to Fred Mann, then acting chief of the OILSR, urging that these and other facts be added to the property reports and that several existing statements be clarified. "Charnita's sole concern is profit and the swift sale of all land in the development," wrote Jeffrey A. Ernico, special assistant attorney-general. "Consequently, consumers are in need of the most meaningful and complete disclosure."

Three months later OILSR decided that Charnita had in fact failed to disclose the building restrictions properly. The agency took unprecedented action: it ordered the developer to offer refunds to 158 persons who bought lots between October 1, 1971, and January 6, 1972, when a statement about the restrictions was added to Charnita's property reports. There was no public announcement of the order; reporters were tipped off to it by private sources. When they made inquiries at HUD, they were told that Charnita had merely committed a "technical violation." One news reporter was told by Larry Beckerman, a HUD public information officer: "Sometimes it's better that these negotiations aren't disclosed." He didn't explain why.

The Charnita case is but one example of the federal regulatory program's deficiencies. As early as 1970 it was apparent that the new law was having only limited impact. "Phony land schemes are booming again," a national newsletter reported. Said the *National Observer:* "Deceptive practices have again become widespread despite new federal restrictions — and at a time when growing numbers of moderate-income people are investing in land as they would in securities, mutual funds, or retirement plans."

Between April, 1969, and the beginning of 1972 OILSR received more than 2,000 written complaints from disgruntled land buyers, and two injunctions were obtained against developers. No developer was fined or sent to jail. There were only a handful of administrative hearings. The rights of five developers to sell in interstate commerce were suspended.

"I admit it's not the most outstanding record of prosecution," said Roy P. Cookston, a lawyer from Dallas, Texas, who succeeded Lehtonen as head of the agency. Cookston complained, with justification, that OILSR's resources are hopelessly inadequate for its immense mission. It has a staff of 42 — including two field investigators — and an annual budget of about $700,000. (The SEC has 1,416 personnel and spent nearly $25 million during its last fiscal year.)

A land buyer who looks to OILSR for protection or assistance should understand clearly what that agency does *not* do. It does not pass on the quality of land offerings. It does *not* inspect subdivisions or verify statements made in registration statements or property reports unless it believes them to be inaccurate. It does *not* require subdividers to post bonds guaranteeing improvements. Except in cases where subdividers fail to register or otherwise comply with the law, OILSR cannot prohibit sales of land no matter how overpriced or unfair the offering may seem. The agency usually does not pass judgment on advertising.

"It should be reemphasized that the [land sales] act is simply and clearly a *disclosure* statute," declares Cookston. "It does not regulate. It does not require anything of a land developer other than to 'tell it like it is.' "

So why do so many developers continue to tell it like it isn't? One reason is that property reports frequently omit, or fail to explain clearly, information that could be crucial in assessing the value of a piece of property as a speculative investment. OILSR could require developers to include such data, since the federal law stipulates that property reports "shall also contain such other information that the Secretary [of Housing and Urban Development — presently George Romney] may by rules or regulations require as being necessary or appropriate in the public interest or for the protection of purchasers."

But the OILSR's regulatory philosophy seems to foreclose the inclusion of such added data.

As a result of great industry pressure, Congress decreed that HUD could accept state regulatory programs as meeting the federal requirements, and thus it is that Florida, New York, California, and Hawaii run their own operations.

Not surprisingly, reports for undeveloped acreage offerings in Florida tell even less than OILSR's. Florida's property reports for undeveloped acreage are silent about the availability of drinking water and the cost of draining or filling. No doubt sales would nosedive if swamp merchants had to admit that removing water from their property would cost millions of dollars. Furthermore, Florida property reports make no mention of whether a particular tract can be drained or whether it is suitable for construction.

A comparison of Florida's disclosure with California's is instructive. Here are some excerpts from a random sampling of California offering statements:

"The prospect of substantial development in the near future is remote. . . . It may be difficult for an individual purchaser to net from the resale of his lot as much as his purchase price. . . . Costs to install a well and pressure system could exceed $2,000" — from a report on Whispering Pines Estates, in Deschutes County, Oregon.

A report on Sun-West Acres, unit number 2, in Mohave County, Arizona, states: "This property is undeveloped raw high desert land and . . . the subdivider has not shown that the parcels can be used for any purpose. . . . To install an individual well with pump . . . will cost over $10,000. . . . All repair and maintenance [of roads] will be at the . . . expense of parcel owners."

Reports for many offerings, including City Estates number 23
in San Bernardino County, California, declare that lot purchasers may have trouble selling their property since they will not
have a sales organization; thus they may find themselves in competition with the subdivider. Califonia's reports include the assessed value of lots and tell how the actual current value can be
computed from these figures. California authorities say that
such disclosure requirements have gone a long way toward protecting the state's residents from swindles. California's already
stringent regulations were strengthened again in 1971. Among
other things, the period of time in which a buyer can cancel a
contract was increased to 14 days.

As we have seen, OILSR publicly boasts that its consumer-
protection activities compare favorably with those of the SEC.
Comparisons again are enlightening. In late 1970 GAC Properties Credit, Inc., a subsidiary of GAC Corporation, issued a
securities prospectus for an offering of 12 percent senior de-
benture bonds. The prospectuses, which conformed with SEC
regulations, revealed that enactment of the truth-in-lending
act "required changes in selling procedures, starting in July
1969, which have had the effect of increasing the rate of contract
cancellations in the early contract months." During the first
nine months of 1970 disillusioned purchasers stopped making
payments on more than $38 million of GAC property.

The prospectuses also contained this illuminating statement:
"There is no significant resale for installment contracts."

None of this information appears in property reports for GAC
land offerings. Buyers of GAC securities consequently are provided with far more information than buyers of its real estate.
(This is almost always the case with subdivision offerings.) A
securities prospectus not only must disclose adverse information about a company or its product but it must disclose it
prominently, in detail, and in understandable terms.

Land buyers as a rule are less sophisticated than securities
buyers, yet property reports are usually filled with legal jargon
that is nearly incomprehensible to the untrained eye. Consider

this example from the offering statement for Rio Grande Estates, one of the Horizon Corporation's subdivisions in New Mexico:

Q: Could the developer's creditors or others acquire title to the property free of any obligation to deliver a deed to the buyer when final payment has been made under the sales contract?

A: Yes. A creditor extending credit without actual notice of the sales contract, a subsequent bona fide purchaser without actual notice of the sales contract and others such as a bona fide purchaser at a judicial sale, could acquire title superior to that of the unrecorded purchaser and therefore would not have the obligation to deliver a deed to the purchaser upon final payment under the sales contract. (This statement is not applicable to a purchaser at a judicial sale of the Deeds of Trust in 5a-g below mentioned because of the subordination provisions.) The developer is current in all its obligations of purchase, and it has lot release credits which it has not exercised.

That means, simply, that if Horizon fails to pay its bills, many of its customers could lose their investments. A securities prospectus would state it that way. Land prospectuses typically contain a good deal of legalistic mumbo jumbo. Unlike securities prospectuses, land prospectuses do not follow a standard form.

The OILSR's contention that land sales regulation resembles securities regulation is as phony as some of the claims of swamp merchants, and the agency is aware of the fact that abuses are rampant. During 1970 and 1971 a Washington, D.C., television newscaster, John Goldsmith of WTTG-TV, broadcast a 25-part series of reports on practices of developers in Virginia, Maryland, and Pennsylvania. Articles on the subject were published by the *Washington Post,* the *Washington Star,* the *Baltimore Sun,* the *Washingtonian,* and several national publications, including the *National Observer, Nation* and *Saturday Review.*

I asked Alfred Lehtonen during this period if he wished to comment on the reports. "There's just *no way* that this law can give further protection to gullible buyers," he snapped. "We're not babysitting with the public. We'll never be able to hold people's hands when they sign a contract."

A short time after making that statement Lehtonen left the government to accept a much better-paying job — as vice-president and general counsel of Horizon Corporation. During Lehtonen's reign at OILSR Horizon's sales volume soared from $36 million to $58 million a year. Remarked Lehtonen's new boss, Horizon vice-president Russell Wilde: "You have a very normal case of a capable executive being seduced out of government."

Lehtonen's departure was followed by that of Herbert H. George, director of administrative proceedings, who went to work as associate general counsel for the American Land Development Association (ALDA). "His areas of activity with ALDA will be reporting on government agency activity and working closely with state government officials," announced the ALDA newsletter, *Washington Developments*.

The first four directors of Florida's regulatory boards quit to work for the land sales industry. John W. McWhirter, Jr., and Carl A. Bertoch opened private law practices with developer clients. Thomas J. Murphy, who came after Bertoch, left to start a land sales consulting business. Lowell Steve, who followed Murphy, joined Nortek, Inc., the Providence, Rhode Island, company that acquired Webb Realty and subsequently ran afoul of New York state authorities. At least three California regulators left to join the land industry.

To be sure, it is not uncommon in Washington for regulators to have a cozy relationship with those they regulate. Unlike OILSR some agencies have responded to the consumer movement by starting to show some real muscle. Among notable examples are the Federal Trade Commission (FTC) and the Food and Drug Administration (FDA). Dedicated consumer champions such as Ralph Nader and his growing band of disciples deserve much of the credit for such salubrious changes of posture. On the other hand, the Nixon administration has not shown any passionate interest in ejecting rascals from the marketplace. The public was forewarned of this attitude during Nixon's 1968 election campaign. In a letter to a group of Wall Street securities brokers Nixon promised that if elected he would put an end to what he termed the "heavy-handed" regulation of the securities industry that, he said, marked the Kennedy and Johnson years. In 1969 the *Wall Street Journal* reported that Nixon "is making good on last September's pledge, and not just for the securities industry but for business in general."

In 1970 *Business Week* called for drastic reforms of the major agencies, noting that they receive "only fitful support from the White House." U.S. Senator Frank E. Moss (D-Utah), chairman of the Senate Commerce Committee's consumer subcommittee, charged that the "Nixon Administration's consumer protection program is a fraud." Columnist Jack Anderson wrote: "President Nixon has faithfully kept a campaign pledge, given privately to fat cat contributors, that he would ease the government's regulation of their businesses. Quietly, he has filled the vacancies on the regulatory agencies with reluctant regulators, who are supposed to protect the public but who have shown more inclination to protect the special interests."

Nixon's unusual relationship with George Smathers, an ultra-conservative Democrat, may shed some light on the president's regulatory philosophy, particularly in the area of land sales. It will be recalled that Smathers derided the idea of federal land sales regulation at the 1964 hearings despite incontrovertible proof that countless people, including many elderly ones (Smathers was then chairman of the Committee on Aging) were being victimized.

As author Sherrill observed, Smathers has always been enthusiastic about land promotion. A noted champion of special interests, the former senator* has been involved in a number of land deals himself. He was a partner in a central Florida land venture with Robert G. (Bobby) Baker, the former secretary to the U.S. Senate majority. In 1967 Baker was convicted of theft, tax evasion, and conspiracy and was sentenced to from one to three years imprisonment. The charges grew out of various extracurricular dealings during his career as Senate secretary but not the one involving Smathers.

---

* The state of Florida lost Smathers's Senate services in 1969. Singed by the Bobby Baker scandal and beleaguered by other embarrassing difficulties, he chose not to run for reelection in 1968 and withdrew from public life.

Smathers was present at groundbreaking ceremonies for the Central Florida Industrial Park near Orlando, where he declared that he would "do anything I can to help it along" — as well he might since he owned part of it. By a remarkable piece of good fortune for the park's investors the Sunshine State Parkway, which had originally been planned to go several miles south of the facility, was rerouted right by it despite the fact that rights of way in the congested Orlando area were much more costly than those along the more southerly route.

More recently it came to light that "the South's Golden Hatchetman," as author Sherrill called Smathers, is a director of and stockholder in Major Realty Corporation, a land wholesaler and developer whose fortunes skyrocketed with the advent of Disney World, south of Orlando. Major Realty has a 3,000-acre development about five miles from the Disney site. Smathers's stock in the company — 94,000 shares — was valued at more than $1 million in 1972. He was named to Major Realty's board in November, 1968, while he was still in the Senate. Public records do not show the circumstances of his stock acquisitions.

Smathers and Nixon have been chummy for more than two decades, and it was Smathers who introduced Nixon to the man who became the president's closest confidant — Charles G. (Bebe) Rebozo. Rebozo had made a good deal of money in the tire-recapping business during World War II, and Nixon had been a lawyer in the tire-rationing division of the Office of Price Administration before entering the navy. A three-cornered friendship developed, and soon Nixon, Smathers, and Rebozo were entering profitable business deals together.

Prior to his election as president, Nixon, with the help of Smathers and Rebozo, acquired a large block of stock in Fisher's Island, Inc., which owns 90 percent of an island in Miami's Bay of Biscayne. That stock, reported *Newsday*, constituted "the bulk of his [Nixon's] declared personal assets" when he entered the White House.

Smathers is a stockholder in the Fisher's Island corporation, and Rebozo is president and treasurer. "Many of the people who own stock in Fisher's Island, Inc., are members of a group of Democratic bankers and businessmen who have long been tied to the investment and election efforts of former Senator Smathers," *Newsday* reported. "The group is widely referred to throughout Florida political spheres as Smathers's 'Goon Squad.' "

In 1971 *Newsday* sent a six-member team of investigative reporters to Florida to look into the "investments and activities" of Rebozo and Smathers "and their relationship with President Nixon." The 65-day probe turned up nothing sensational. The reporters complained that they were repeatedly refused access to records and other information by government agencies, but they documented enough questionable dealings on the part of Smathers and Rebozo to cause *Newsday*'s editors to conclude after a long series of articles: "The deals made by Bebe Rebozo and the Smathers gang have tarnished the Presidency."

In the period since federal authorities began moving into land sales regulation many subdividers have organized themselves into national, regional, and state trade associations. ALDA, created in 1970, is the largest such group. Developers accounting for about 45 percent of the recreational land sales in California — among them units of Transamerica Corporation, Dart Industries, Inc., Tenneco, Inc., and Avco Corporation — formed the Western Developers Council in October, 1970. "One apparent — but unstated — purpose," the *Wall Street Journal* reported, is "to head off state legislation that would switch land-planning controls from local agencies to state authorities." Local authorities often aren't very strict with developers, a fact that many Californians have complained about.

Other regional organizations include Rocky Mountain Developers Association, Pennsylvania Vacation Land Developers Association, and New England Land Developers Association. State associations have been formed in Virginia, Texas, and Michigan.

There is also a National Land Council, Inc., based in Tampa, Florida, and headed by Carl Bertoch, the former land board director. That group's principal mission is "the establishment of uniformity" in federal, state, and local land sales regulations. Its membership includes officials of General Development Corporation, Grand Bahama Development Corporation, AMREP Corporation, and ITT Community Development Corporation. Alfred Lehtonen, representing Horizon Corporation, is a director, and W. Patrick Green, a member of Morton Rothenberg's Miami Beach law firm, is a member.

In late 1971 ALDA claimed 500 members (5 percent of the industry if the group is correct in its estimate that there are 10,000 active subdividers who sell land in interstate commerce). ALDA members pledge themselves to support a number of lofty aims, including:

> In matters of land development the public good and benefit is to be a major consideration.
>
> Reasonable efforts are to be made to preserve and protect natural flora and fauna peculiar to a region or locale where development may be undertaken.
>
> In the sale or advertisement for sale of land or improvements, fair market value is not to be misstated or misrepresented.

But while professing strong support for consumer protection ALDA, which is registered as a Washington lobbying organization, has fought legislation that would provide the two things that leading consumer advocates want most — an independent federal office of consumer affairs and authority under which consumers could band together and institute class-action lawsuits against business firms in an attempt to redress wrongs. ALDA is not likely to look kindly on proposals that may be made for regulating the industry with a heavier hand. Through its monthly newsletter, *Washington Developments,* ALDA alerts its members to all legislative proposals that could affect land subdividers. One issue of the publication took several unnamed newspapers to task for publishing unfavorable reports about land developers; ALDA bemoaned the fact that association officials had tried to reason with reporters but to no avail.

ALDA sponsors meetings, workshops, and seminars thoughout the country, including an annual land conference. The guest roster of the 1971 conference included such notables as HUD Secretary Romney, Robert Trent Jones, Jr., the golf course architect, and Roy Cookston. Nearly 700 subdividers were on hand for what *Washington Developments* described as "the largest single gathering in the history of the land industry." The air was filled with ringing oratory. Fred Roach, president of General Development, said the conclave marked a "new era" for the industry, and he predicted a "shifting emphasis" away from the development of retirement communities toward such creations as theme parks and recreation vehicle centers. W. John Duncan, president of ALDA, urged the delegates to continue to upgrade the industry's products.

There were some less sanguine moments at the conference. Cookston reported that complaints against subdividers lodged with OILSR had doubled in the preceding year. George Romney said that the "most important thing" that ALDA could do would be "to undertake self-policing." Columnist Jack Anderson warned that the industry would not survive unless it "developed a conscience."

By 1972 — a presidential election year — OILSR's impotence was being made ever more obvious by a swelling profusion of state and private actions against developers. Calling for "tough, meaningful regulation," Secretary Romney assigned George K. Bernstein, the federal insurance administrator, to the additional job of running OILSR (Cookston had left months before). A burst of activity followed.

Five OILSR employees were transferred. The agency decreed that henceforth developers operating within state boundaries would be required to register; this raised the estimated number of subdividers under OILSR's jurisdiction from 3,500 to 10,000.

In March, Bernstein halted sales at Charnita (see Chapter 5). In April, he announced the first criminal prosecution under the federal land-sales law — a grand jury in Kansas City, Missouri, charged developer Robert V. Steinhilber with making false statements on property reports for two developments in Cass County, Missouri: Lake Winnebago and Lake Winnebago

South. Bernstein served notice that more prosecutions could be expected. OILSR began pushing for amendments designed to strengthen the federal law.

By May, the new administrator had concluded that "thousands of people every week are being misled or cheated when buying lots for recreational, retirement, or investment purposes." To ascertain the extent of the skulduggery, Bernstein scheduled public hearings in 16 cities during the spring and summer. He said, "We're going throughout the country to find out what problems they [land buyers] are having and to indentify the fast-talking, silver-tongued sharpies who are causing those problems.

"For far too long, the fast-talking, silver-tongued sharpies . . . have been using methods that are improper and often illegal." The hearings, he added, should lead to "greater public awareness, to further legal action, to improved regulatory procedures, and, if necessary, to . . . better statutory protection."

It was tough talk. If it is matched with appropriate action, Bernstein will have performed public service of inestimable value.

12

Raping the Land
of Enchantment

Iɴ an article entitled "Land Peddlers Wrecking
the West," published by the *Denver Post,* former U.S. Interior
Secretary Stewart L. Udall wrote in 1970:

> "Land speculations are rapidly foreclosing the expansion op-
> tions in the fast-growing states of the Southwest. . . . This is an en-
> vironmental disaster of major proportions. It is sabotaging a wa-
> ter-short region that desperately needs orderly growth and well-
> planned communities if it is to protect the fragile environment
> . . . . Irreparable damage has already been done. But if the slow-
> footed legislators and public officials don't act soon, they may find
> the cities surrounded by ghost towns gouged into the desert top-
> soil while the super-developers laugh all the way back to their
> eastern banks."

This was no exaggeration. By 1972 the situation had worsened,
and profits of the super-developers had scaled new heights. Yet
legislators, for the most part, remained as slow-footed as ever.

188

Why? What is it that enables subdividers to rape the land-scape and rook the public almost at will?

New Mexico, a state that Udall described as being "under siege by speculators," provides a fascinating case study.

In 1971 New Mexico's Environmental Improvement Agency estimated conservatively that well over one million acres of rural rangeland, mesas, and desert had been staked out in build-ing lots — enough to house up to 8 million persons. The state's population in 1970 totaled 1,016,000; in 1972 the Bureau of Economic Analysis of the U.S. Department of Commerce esti-mated that only about 1,336,000 persons will live in New Mexi-co by the year 2000. (The Bureau of Business Research at the University of New Mexico calculates that the total could go as high as 2.8 million.)

The subdividing frenzy has even spread to Indian lands. The fact that Indian reservations are owned by the government didn't deter the developers of Colonias de Santa Fe and Co-chiti Lake. In cooperative ventures with Indian tribes the com-panies are *leasing* land from the Indians for 99 years and sub-leasing lots to the public.

Nobody, including the subdividers themselves, expects all of the lots that have been platted to be used as homesites. A significant percentage of the parcels are bought as speculative investments, and many are uninhabitable. "I refuse to believe the population will ever reach the level of purchases," declares former State Representative Carter Kirk, president of Select Western Lands, Inc.

But trouble could occur if only a fraction of the properties are homesteaded. Water is scarce in many places. According to law all users except owners of single-family dwellings must buy "water rights." Underground water tables have fallen in recent years as much as 100 feet west and south of Santa Fe. Rationing was necessary there in 1971.

In short, nobody knows how much additional population the water supply will support.

There are other reasons why the state may have difficulty ab-sorbing a large influx of newcomers: New Mexico has had a high unemployment rate and a low per-capita income; it lacks a diversified economy; its resources are limited; and a large segment of its present population has few skills. Although the Land of Enchantment, as New Mexico calls itself, is noted for its salubrious climate and clean air, the specter of atmospheric pollution is already causing nervousness in Albuquerque. "If the population doubled, we'd have a critical pollution problem," warns Michael Connolly, a meteorologist in the Air Management Division of the city's Environmental Health Department. "The problem is serious now — and it's getting worse."

To make known their antipathy to uncontrolled growth many motorists have begun to display bumper stickers saying "Save the Valley," "Undevelop," "Our National Product is Gross," and "Save the Environment — Leave."

Even without people, however, the subdivisions are causing big headaches. Over 8,000 miles of dirt roads have been gouged in the beige-colored earth. Subdividers in New Mexico are required by law to provide road access to lots. "The aerial view of New Mexico today is studded with surrealistic checkerboards of dirt roads carved in the empty countryside," wrote Bill Hume, state editor of the *Albuquerque Journal*.

Dust from the roads is a major cause of air pollution. In wet weather erosion occurs. "Thousands of acres of prime New Mexico land have been destroyed," says Dr. Cynthia Irwin-Williams, a professor of anthropology at Eastern New Mexico University. "The topsoil is being removed, and the normal vegetation won't return until the year 2000. The roads have created scars and destroyed land which will never come back in our lifetime. The land couldn't support one million people."

For counties in which the roads are located there is the possibility of having to pay future maintenance costs. A study by the city planning department in Santa Fe found that tax revenue from new suburban subdivisions there paid only about 80 percent of the costs of maintenance and other services provided by the city. City taxpayers made up the difference.

Roads in rural subdivisions usually follow simple grid patterns of the type detested by land planners because of monotony and lack of open space. The better suburban developments have more aesthetic appeal; they usually include parks, golf courses, and varied street patterns, but even they are programmed for maximum profit. In a 1971 editorial the *Journal* observed:

> It was neither planners nor nature nor availability of jobs that dictated the location of Rio Rancho Estates, or Santa California City, or all the other romantically named plots of New Mexico being sold an acre at a time. Their locations were determined instead by the economics of available land, by the profit motives of mostly out-of-state businessmen. New Mexico deserves better. The location of new population centers should be determined by the collective judgment of the best trained minds available rather than the profit motive of private nonresident businessmen.

Moreover, the tactics used to sell lots bother many residents. "We hate to see people get rooked," bristles Lloyd Barlow, an urban planner with Albuquerque's city planning department. The *Albuquerque Journal* stated: "In the past decade the activities of land developers have probably brought more adverse publicity to New Mexico than any other topic." The paper said further, "The state's reputation has been blemished, and land titles on large blocks have been confused beyond all imagination." Land prices have been artificially inflated, driving up housing costs.

In short, all of the evils of premature subdividing have been visited on New Mexico to a dismaying degree. New Mexico is regarded by some observers as the quintessential example of a state ravaged by land hustlers.

In 1971 the *Journal* called for statewide subdivision controls and recommended the enactment of legislation "so strong" that "it effectively brings to a halt the sale of tiny parcels of land in water-short areas." Nothing happened.

In 1972 the reform-seekers tried a new tack, lining up behind a bill to require developers of new subdivisions to prove to the satisfaction of state authorities that enough underground water would be available to meet the needs of the anticipated population. The measure was intended as emergency stop-gap to check excessive subdividing at least until statewide land planning could be inaugurated.

The proposition seemed reasonable enough. After all, a waterless "homesite" has little value. "They [the reform bloc] became convinced that the most politically realistic way to establish control [over new subdivisions] was to require that subdividers provide water with their land, something many of them would clearly not be able to do," a group of 13 law students at the University of New Mexico later wrote in an analysis of the legislative contest.

The bill was endorsed by Governor Bruce King, Attorney-General David Norvell, State Engineer S.E. Reynolds, the state's leading newspapers, and an array of organizations including the New Mexico League of Women Voters, the Sierra Club, Citizens Coalition for Land-Use Planning, New Mexico Conservation Coordinating Council, Friends of the Earth, New Mexico Citizens for Clean Air and Water, the New Mexico Soil and Conservation Association, and the Albuquerque chapter of the American Institute of Architects.

The lobbying effort was spearheaded by the Central Clearing House (CCH), a Santa Fe-based congress of conservation groups headed by Harvey Mudd, a Taos, New Mexico, resident who inherited a family copper-mining fortune and uses part of it to help finance conservation causes. "The present situation is an emergency," warned Mudd.

Mike Williams, a member of Governor King's Environmental Quality Council, was even more emphatic. "I consider it [land subdivision] to be our biggest environmental problem."

A poll conducted in southern New Mexico, a conservative region, by the state's Republican party showed that citizens there favored statewide land use controls by a margin of 8 to 1.

Members of the Central Clearing House spent nine months before the legislature convened pleading their cause with legislators, subdividers, realtors, and anyone else who would listen.

"We thought nearly everybody was with us," relates Sally Rodgers, executive director of the organization. "The big subdividers said that they'd go along."

Then the subdividers' lobby went to work, and the bill was defeated.

It was a bombastic struggle. When the dust settled, State Representative James Koch (D-Santa Fe), a strong advocate of the bill, murmured with awe: "The subdividers' lobby is the strongest I've ever seen up here. It's stronger than the liquor lobby ever was. It's stronger than the truck lobby. These people [the subdividers] showed absolutely no willingness to work, compromise . . . and the result of this is going to be in the very near future, and their representatives are going to run over them, and they'll deserve every bit of it."

The lobby included the Realtors Association of New Mexico, the Albuquerque Home Builders Association, and many cattlemen who feared that the bill would foreclose any opportunity that they might have to sell their ranches for subdivision.

The Realtors Association is an affiliate of the National Association of Real Estate Boards, which continually publicizes the fact that members must ascribe to a code of ethics. Article 3 of that code states:

> It is the duty of the realtor to protect the public against fraud, misrepresentation, or unethical practices in the real estate field. He should endeavor to eliminate in his community any practices which could be damaging to the public or to the dignity and integrity of the profession.

During the legislative session the New Mexico association hosted a cocktail party at a local motel with an invitation to members of the legislature. A member of the group offered to raise $30,000 to $50,000 to "finance a year's study" of subdividing practices. Mudd declined. But the realtors got their wish; the legislature authorized the appointment of an 11-member committee to study the problems and to recommend corrective legislation prior to the 1973 session.

Representatives of the major subdividers swarmed through the capital during the debate on the subdivision bill. On hand for Horizon Corporation, which controls at least 175,000 acres in New Mexico, was its vice-president and general counsel, Alfred J. Lehtonen, the former federal regulator. AMREP

Corporation, which has some 91,000 acres, flew its vice-president and general counsel, Sol Friend, in for the session.

Southwest Land Corporation, Greatwestern Cities, and D. W. Falls, Inc. also made their presence felt. Fred Standley, attorney for Colonias de Santa Fe, was particularly active in opposition to the measure.

The debate was charged with virulence. "Their avowed intent is to stop all subdivisions, including all new ones, in the state," snapped Carter Kirk, of Select Western Lands, who previously conceded that more land was being sold than would be used. State Senator Eddie Barboa (D-Bernalillo) exclaimed: "I don't see why we should spend hours worrying about somebody in New York spending $1,500 or $2,000 on a worthless piece of New Mexico land. If they're that stupid, let them do it."

Afterward Sally Rodgers reflected: "We were threatened, offered bribes, intimidated, and betrayed. They used smear tactics and personal attacks. It was vicious and extraordinarily dishonest. But they won."

Harvey Mudd attributed the defeat to conflicts of interest. The subdivision control battle focused attention on the fact that several of New Mexico's most prominent political figures are associated with subdividers, do business with them, or are subdividers themselves.

Prior to taking office Governor King and his brothers Don and Sam sold several thousand acres of ranchland to AMREP. While he was a member of the legislature, Bruce King appeared in a promotional film for AMREP's Rio Rancho Estates development and delivered this spiel:

> Hi, I'm Bruce King, speaker of the New Mexico House of Representatives, State Representative of Santa Fe County. And it certainly is a pleasure to appear here this morning on this beautiful spot and view the Sandia Mountains to the east of us and the large metropolitan area of over 300,000 people. And I'm sure that in the next two decades we will expand much more, and the city of Albuquerque will overflow and come right in the path of where we are standing this morning. And it will no doubt be a

million people in the next two decades. The population of America is expanding, but they don't make any more land.

The governor's support of the subdivision control bill — in fulfillment of a campaign pledge — was not distinguished by vigor.

Don King is chairman of the Santa Fe County Commission. In 1971 he pushed for approval of a plat for a new 27,000-acre AMREP development, El Dorado at Santa Fe, despite a lack of evidence that adequate water could be obtained. His fellow commissioners balked, and only 2,000 acres received initial approval.

Horizon's legal counsel in New Mexico is Turner Branch, of Bernalillo, a member of the state's House of Representatives. He voted for several debilitating amendments to the subdivision bill.

The advertising agent for Colonias de Santa Fe is Edmunde Delgade, of Santa Fe, a member of the State Senate. He voted for a powerless substitute subdivision bill, which died in committee when backers of the original legislation refused to support it.

The original measure failed to pass "because of these and other legislative conflicts of interest," the Central Clearing House charged in a formal statement. In their 29-page analysis of the legislative fight University of New Mexico law students concluded that "conflict of interest" was "probably an insurmountable bar to fair, effective subdivision legislation" in the 1972 session.

"It became obvious to those of us who followed the legislation that the real aim of the subdividers was to have no control," the students wrote. "They proved that, at least for now, they have a stranglehold on this state and the people who govern it." As for legislators who are beholden to developers, the group said, "It is clearly up to the voters to rise up as one angry citizen and throw the bounders out."

New Mexico Architecture, a magazine published by the New Mexico Society of Architects fumed: "It is tantamount to disaster for us to continue to allow the self-interest of large land development companies to serve only their own stockholders, with little or no consideration for the long-range impact that their short-range goals have upon the future environment of New Mexico. To continue to despoil our own air with soot, to continue to 'develop' productive crop land and grazing land into poorly planned retirement 'ranchettes' is to court an eventual ecological catastrophe."

Advocates of subdivision controls vowed to fight on. They formed a new organization, the Citizens Environmental Campaign Fund, in an attempt to "change the complexion of the legislature" by working for the election of reform-minded candidates and the defeat of certain incumbents. "The people will have an opportunity . . . to change this outrageous situation by electing men and women who will truly represent *them*," said Harvey Mudd. The CCH published a fact-filled brochure about New Mexico land and distributed several thousand copies around the country "so that at least some people will learn the truth," Sally Rodgers said.

In Deming, New Mexico, the Luna County Commission adopted a new policy under which it will "deny the use of all county road building, maintenance, and accessory equipment to subdivision roads and access roads until such a time as fully warranted by population density and tax base." And the Southwest New Mexico Resource Conservation and Development Project, a conservation group that counts the governor's office and some state agencies as members, requested several national publications to be more selective in accepting advertisements for New Mexico land.

For instance, the *National Observer* and *Parade* magazine received letters from A. D. Brownfield, Jr., chairman of the group's steering committee, regarding ads for offerings of Select Western Lands, Inc. The letters listed numerous difficulties that lot buyers could expect to encounter but that weren't mentioned in the advertising — difficulties with obtaining water, disposing of waste, building a home on land on which special construction techniques must be used because of stress patterns affecting the soil, and living in an area where there is alkaline soil, little vegetation, frequent high winds, and thunderstorms that sometimes leave houses surrounded by water for several months.

"In this particular instance, the natural resources of the area are being destroyed, and thousands of investors will eventually lose millions of dollars, as will future taxpayers," Brownfield wrote. "I therefore implore you to deny acceptance of all such advertising in the future and to use as much of your great influence as possible in the establishment of such a policy by all major publishing houses as your own."

The *Albuquerque Journal* allowed: "It is obvious that the members of the legislature completely misread the public pulse in the area of subdivision controls and will be hearing from the public in the future."

That seemed to be a safe prediction.

In 1971 a bomb exploded in the Colonias sales office, shattering its front. No one was injured, but the cause of the violence wasn't determined. Also that year, the developers filed a $2.5 million damage suit against the CCH and another environmental group, the Santa Fe Area Defense Fund, charging the defendants with conspiring to interfere with business.

13

Land Hustlers and the Press

No institution has done more to expose phony land-sales schemes than the press. And yet, some members of the fourth estate unwittingly aid and abet malpractices. Here are some examples.

In its April 14, 1963, issue, the *Orlando Sentinel* carried a full-length story about Rocket City, a hotly promoted land offering between Orlando and Cape Kennedy. On the cover of the Sunday supplement was a color picture of John B. Medaris, a retired army general, standing in front of a huge billboard that bore the words: "ROCKET CITY Urban/Suburban Complex. Make It Yours for a Brighter Tomorrow." The article, head-lined "GO for Rocket City," related how "Army troubleshooter Medaris tackles the task of getting a 36-square-mile land development off the ground." Illustrated with pictures of giant draglines, bulldozers, and drainage canals, the piece described how a vast stretch of scrubby, swampy boondocks was being transformed into a metropolis. Medaris was proclaimed as the *Sentinel's* "Man of the Week," a title that the newspaper regularly bestows on distinguished citizens in the area (and sometimes on advertisers). Medaris, who had set up the Ballistic Missile Agency in Huntsville, Alabama, had on retirement become board chairman of All-State Development Corporation, the developer of Rocket City.

For All-State the *Sentinel* publicity was priceless. The layout immediately became part of the exhibits used by Rocket City's sales force. It undoubtedly impressed many of the 2,500 persons who bought lots in the subdivision, which was touted far and wide as "the new planned-for-tomorrow metropolis in the making. . .in the fastest-growing area of our fast-growing state. . .directly in the path of booming space-age progress. . .and offering unsurpassed opportunity for the small investor!"

Rocket City indeed took off but in the wrong direction. First troubleshooter Medaris bailed out, evidently sensing more trouble ahead than he or anyone else could overcome.* Florida authorities were deluged with complaints about All-State's sales tactics. Soon afterward the corporation ran short of cash and was besieged by creditors. In 1965 its license to sell real estate was revoked by the Florida Installment Land Sales Board because of deceptive selling and inability to finance promised improvements. Orange County Solicitor James G. Horrell reported that an investigation by his office disclosed evidence of "waste of funds, extravagance, careless accounting methods, extremely high pressure and questionable methods of salesmanship, and possibly fraud on the public."

---

*Medaris was not implicated in the events that followed. It appears that he was only a figurehead, hired because of the prestige value of his name. Celebrities have helped to promote land sales since William Jennings Bryan held forth on the splendors of Coral Gables. Years ago the resonant voice of Bill Stern, the sportscaster, filled the sound tracks of Gulf American sales films. Today, big names associated with land offerings include those of Chet Huntley, Anita Bryant, and Don McNeill.

All-State filed for bankruptcy in 1966. In 1969 a federal Grand Jury indicted Milton M. Mendelsohn, the president and general manager of All-State, and three others on 25 counts of mail fraud and conspiracy to defraud. Mendelsohn's trial, held in 1970, ended in a mistrial. The Justice Department then authorized the charges to be dropped. In Baltimore in 1970 Mendelsohn pleaded guilty of violating federal registration requirements in the selling of All-State stock and was sentenced to one year's imprisonment. He admitted devising a scheme that caused 400 people to invest in All-State. Mendelsohn's lawyers said that no swindle was intended; they termed Rocket City's demise as the collapse of a "risky" venture.

Intended swindle or not, Rocket City was a $3.1-million fiasco that left a lot of people poorer, and the *Sentinel* was an unwitting accessory. No doubt the newspaper's editors, like General Medaris, sincerely felt that the undertaking could be a rousing success and that a bit of help in the form of free publicity could harm no one. But a little investigating might have changed their minds. Had they investigated, they would have learned, among other things, that the scheme was thinly financed, that creditors were already uneasy, that draining the property might be economically unfeasible, that blatant deception was being used in the selling of lots, and that the Orange County Commission had refused to approve new plats for the development without adequate financial security, which All-State did not provide.

It is not at all unusual for newspapers to aid questionable land promotions by according them favorable publicity — a supreme irony in face of the efforts of some members of the press, especially certain newspapers, to expose shady land promotions and to preach the gospel of strict regulation. The honor roll of papers that have distinguished themselves in this respect is a long one, including the *Miami Herald*, the *Wall Street Journal*, the *National Observer*, the *Daytona Beach News-Journal*, the *Albuquerque Journal*, the *St. Petersburg Times*, the *Arizona Republic*, the *Tucson Star*, the *Washington*

Star, the *Newark Evening News,* and the *Eugene Register-Guard.* The *Miami Herald* has been lambasting swamp merchants for more than two decades, and the *Wall Street Journal,* the reader will recall, pried loose the long-suppressed report on Gulf-American Corporation's misbehavior.

While some papers are ever ready to attack iniquities, others are not. Even some of the best publications are sometimes flummoxed by glib real estate promoters, often because staff members are inexperienced or editors fail to allow sufficient time for investigation. As *Time* magazine once noted, in the pecking order of many newspapers' editorial offices the real estate editor ranks about one rung above the fellow who writes about high school sports events.

All too often the realty beat goes to a neophyte or to somebody who couldn't make it covering crime or politics. In many an otherwise good news sheet the real estate section is little more than a repository for canned releases and publicity puffs from advertisers. Many a honeyed article has been planted by a press agent or written by somebody on the news staff who was wined, dined, and brainwashed by a developer.

Early in 1972 Senator Frank Moss (D-Utah) directed the staff of his Senate consumer subcommittee to investigate the extent to which reporters and editors accept payoffs in return for publicity. In a confidential memo Moss said that journalists who cover news about real estate, automobiles, household furnishings, travel, food, and pharmaceutical products are especially prone to corruption. "When I see automotive reporters using the same words to attack air bags as Ford uses in its press releases, I am troubled even when the arguments themselves may be valid," said the senator. "When I see language identical to words of a press release in an ostensible news story, I lack the confidence that I am getting a newsman's judgment."

The number of journalists who could be adjudged actually corrupt is minute. Still, there are some who are overawed by corporate flacks and others who lack the time, background, or expertise to do an adequate job of reporting on a specialized subject such as real estate.

Many of the larger land companies spend great sums of money in courting the news media. For years General Development Corporation staged an annual weekend junket and golf tournament for reporters and editors. Participants would be invited to Port St. Lucie, Florida, a General Development community south of Cape Kennedy, where they would stay in lavish villas. They would be served the best food and drink and treated to two rounds of golf on a championship course.

Deltona Corporation regularly flies planeloads of reporters to its communities for weekend visits. These excursions feature golf, swimming, cocktail parties, plus a few deft injections of soft sell. The newspeople are taken on a tour of the community and invited to chat with residents. If any reporter suspects that the residents are booster types who were trotted out only because they are kindly disposed toward Deltona, he or she is free to interview others — if there is any time for it between social activities.

The cost of such promotional junkets is astronomical, but it pays off. Any favorable stories that result — and many do — are invaluable. Not only can such articles spur sales in a newspaper's circulation area, but they are usually reproduced in sales brochures. Few sales aides are more persuasive than a complimentary newspaper or magazine article.

Granted, there is nothing necessarily wrong with wooing the press. It can be argued, in fact, that only a company with something worthwhile to show off would turn hordes of newspaper reporters loose on its properties. Nevertheless, the press-agentry all too often results in one-sided, panegyrical reportage. Every development has bad points as well as good. Reporters who accept largesse from land companies compromise their integrity, and responsible publishers strictly forbid it.

Many of the larger land development companies employ platoons of ingenious flacks who constantly try to dream up ways of getting free publicity. For example, below are re-

produced excerpts from an interoffice memo distributed in
1970 by Boise Cascade Corporation's Recreation Communities
Group:

> . . .there is *one way* you can pick up *reams* of publicity till we
> have it coming out of our ears — and favorable publicity, too.
> That is to organize a *program*. . .
> It's the *now* way of thinking — the *now* journalism — *what
> editors want!*
> I'm suggest [*sic*] we immediately start at all our projects (we
> could have a test case of one), giving all the project employees
> one morning a week off (but paying them their regular salary):
> (a) to pick up litter on Main Street of, say, Auburn, California;
> (b) another day to pick up litter at town park; (c) another day
> to take paint (we contribute) and paint a town eyesore a la
> Groveland, California.
> By doing this, every week we *create* favorable news, that the
> media can cover and they do the writing and take pix. . . .Local
> press would love us because we'd be furnishing them with *people*-
> type news, lots of names, about the most vital *issue of our day* —
> pollution. . . .If question is raised about our questionable practices,
> we say we're correcting them as fast as possible.

Some of the things that have been written about land
developments sound as though they came right out of the
developer's publicity office. "Florida's Palm Coast Truly a
'New City,'" proclaimed a headline in the *Boston Sunday
Globe* in February, 1971. The authority for that statement, one
learns from reading the article, is Dr. Norman Young, president of ITT Community Development Corporation, developer
of Palm Coast. Young was quoted as saying: "This is to be
the first [community] of its kind in terms of preplanned,
preprogrammed cities, and in order to do this we've engaged
a variety of consultants in the area of city planning, ecology,
behavorial science and education." The story didn't mention
Palm Coast's clash with Florida's environmental authorities.

The *Orlando Sentinel*, evidently unchastened by the Rocket
City fiasco, trumpeted: "Land Sales Soar at Palm Coast."
The story began: "Whether you fly over it, boat through it, or

drive around it, Palm Coast is bound to impress you as one of the most exciting land development undertakings in the history of Florida. How else could one describe 100,000 acres of near virgin land which, within the next 25 to 30 years, is destined to have a population of three-quarters of a million people?" The article wasn't very specific about what was so exciting about the project, but it included a number of Dr. Young's superlatives. At one point he was quoted as saying: "Palm Coast land sales have exceeded our highest expectations. This. . .substantiates the strong belief that land is one of the most substantial forms of investment for many."

U.S. Land, Inc., developer of Lake of the Woods, near Fredericksburg, Virginia, managed to fill a whole brochure with news items about the development, most of them from Washington, D.C., papers. John McKelway, who writes a column for the *Washington Star*, devoted two pieces to the project. "Let's get something straight," he began in the second one. "The Rambler [the name of McKelway's column] is not trying to sell any lots. But he did feel it was necessary to pay another visit to a place called Lake of the Woods." There followed about 600 words of complimentary descriptive prose.

John B. Willmann, real estate editor of the *Washington Post*, one of the *Star*'s rivals, also was taken on a guided tour of Lake of the Woods, but he included in his account a report of the hard selling that went on. The car radio "began squawking," he wrote. "Salesmen with prospects in tow were calling Sales GHQ to inquire if lot number so-and-so was still available. Usually it was. Then a hesitation and the salesman said, 'Mark it sold.' You might hear a woman's voice expressing delight." This went on so long that Willmann "twitted the developers about arranging these reports" to impress him. Later he found that exactly eight sales had been made that day. "Half of those sales must have been recorded between 4:30 and 5:30 p.m.," the editor said.

On March 20, 1970, the *Washington Daily News* carried

a column about Chamisa Ranches, in Arizona, by its real estate editor, Lew Sichelman, headed: "Your Chance to Be a Land Baron." It said, in part: "Now anyone can buy land wholesale at prices usually paid by developers. . . .Offered, indeed, is a rare opportunity — a chance to become a land baron," wrote Sichelman. The subdivider, Ronald Sandler, was quoted at length on the grandeur of the offering. Commented Sichelman: "The area, reputedly one of the most popular in Arizona, where the population is increasing at three times the national average, is in the midst of a land and housing-development boom, according to Sandler." According to *Sandler?* The columnist evidently didn't bother to confirm that statement himself. Sandler liked the column so much that he reprinted it in full and ran it as paid advertising in other newspapers, including the *Washington Post.*

It goes without saying that announcements of real estate ventures and the creation of new communities are usually newsworthy and that the news media have an obligation to report them. But the media's principal obligation is to the public, and that demands factual, informative reportage.

Reporters should ask a few searching questions: How is the project being financed? Have bonds been posted to guarantee improvements? How will the property be merchandised? What are the developers' credentials? Newspapers should keep in mind that anything they print that's even slightly favorable is likely to be preserved in sales literature.

A good deal of healthy skepticism is in order in assessing any announcement of a new real estate undertaking. If the developer later produces a first-rate community, *that* is the time to toss out the bouquets — when they're deserved. The press ought to do anything it can to encourage quality and integrity in community development.

In reporting on land development and real estate in general the press would do better to rely less on the real estate industry for information and more on such sources as government agencies, land-planning experts, regulators, and others who have no vested interest in the image of the real estate business.

Brokers, developers, and land dealers are out to *promote* business. For instance, in a story captioned "Florida's Land Boom Gets Down to Earth," *Business Week* magazine told its readers on April 13, 1968: "Fly-by-night operators of the past have been replaced by big corporations that have the skilled management and capital to put real estate development on a lasting basis." The sources of that information apparently were officers of three land companies — General Development Corporation, Arvida Corporation, and Deltona Corporation.

U. S. News & World Report has published several specials about land buying and rising values. One of them, headed *"The Big Land Rush: No Slowdown in Sight,"* appeared December 13, 1971, and was liberally sprinkled with such quotes as: "We think recreation land is a tremendous growth area. It attracts people who want to use their increased leisure time for recreation, or who want to invest in land for profit, or both." The quote came from a developer — Sabino Marinella, senior vice-president of Continental Investment Corporation of Boston.

O. A. Sokoloski, a Missoula, Montana, real estate developer, was quoted in the same article: "We have a great deal of speculation in Montana land. With the stock market like it is, people feel this is a better investment. I have people call me every time the market flutters. They take their loss on stocks and go to land." H. Richard Ronneburg, vice-president of Strout Realty, Inc., of Pasadena, California, said that "One of the reasons recreational property is in so much demand is that people are afraid it won't be available for them and their children in the years ahead. They can afford to buy it now. In the future they won't have this opportunity, they fear."

There is, of course, nothing wrong with quoting real estate dealers on market conditions or the magnificence of their offerings, but there are other facets of the situation that *U. S. News* did not discuss. What percentage of the sales represents genuine demand and what percentage results from high-pressure or deceptive selling? What about all the people who invested in land in the past and now can't unload it at any price? The truth is that a great deal of land offerings, like a great many shares in mutual funds, are not *bought;* they are *sold,* through highly effective (and often reprehensible) techniques.

Another publication that doesn't seem to have noticed the resurgence of phony land sales schemes is *Barron's,* the business and financial weekly. On June 13, 1966, *Barron's* published a long article that was so euphoric about the Florida land industry that Installment Land Sales and Development Association of Florida, Inc., the "self-policing" industry group, introduced it into the record of hearings on federal land sales legislation that were held that year by a Senate banking subcommittee.

The story led off with this statement by Henry Dubbin, chairman of Canaveral International Corporation, a diversified firm that has sold small tracts of unimproved Florida acreage to many small investors: "Owning a piece of land is a basic part of the American dream. We're giving thousands of Americans a chance to make that dream come true." A short time after the article appeared Dubbin and six others were indicted by a federal Grand Jury on charges of stock manipulation. In 1972 Canaveral International was accused by the Federal Trade Commission of violating the truth-in-lending law in sales of mobile homes. The company signed a consent order in which it agreed to refrain from such infractions thereafter.

The *Barron's* story further said: "The painful scandals that shook the industry a few years ago served to weed out marginal firms, clearing the way for those with well-planted roots. It also produced a crop of new statewide real-estate regulations, further stimulating the strong companies by affording public investors protection against undue risk." A few paragraphs later *Barron's* commented: "In any event, the satisfied customer — and, one day, the happy homeowner — would seem to offer proof that today's methods are not heading the industry into the kind of trouble it's been in before. Says Harry Schloss, Gulf American's treasurer: 'Something like 80 percent of our sales are made to people who have seen what they're buying or who see it within six months. In most of the latter cases, they wind up buying more.'" Almost a year after those words were published, the *Wall Street Journal* disclosed that Gulf American had been accused of "grossly immoral and unethical sales activities" by the staff of the Florida Installment Land Sales Board. As the reader will recall, the company pleaded guilty.

Barron's, however, remained myopic. On March 11, 1968, the publication observed: "Florida's speculative fiascos were built upon shaky finances and shakier ethics. Now that kind of building has all but disappeared from the scene. . . .For the first time, owing mainly to the efforts of Governor Claude Kirk (who last year became the first Republican in the state-house since the Civil War), investors are protected from the shady promotional and selling practices by a land-sales regulatory statute with teeth in it."

As subsequent events have shown, that statement missed the mark by several light years.

Sometimes even the best publications trip over their own rhetoric. On November 2, 1971, the *Wall Street Journal*, which exposed Gulf American Corporation, carried on its editorial page a lengthy critique of Ralph Nader's *Power and Land in California*. The *Journal* piece was written by A. Richard Immel and was headlined: "*Ralph Nader's Shoddy Product.*"

Nader's investigators, asserted Immel, "have come up with a report that is flawed by minor inaccuracies and burdened with its own bias; worse, it is largely irrelevant."

Nine paragraphs later Immel conceded: "Beneath the rhetoric it can't be denied that many, if not most, of the conditions described do exist. But it is also true that most Californians seem aware of these problems and have been for some time."

Immel allowed that the study "does have its strong points. . . .In contrast to the Nader rhetoric, most of the report's recommendations tend to be rational, if sometimes arguable. But most of the major suggestions aren't original. They have been discussed in California and elsewhere for years."

What sort of convoluted reasoning is *that?* Because a subject has been "discussed," it shouldn't be written about? Because a recommendation isn't original, it should be discarded?

A fair-sized segment of the California press likewise assailed the Nader report, often in attacks that amounted to nit-picking at a study that is an important and valuable piece of work. If it does nothing more than provoke discussion — and it assuredly has done that, as the *Journal* piece attests — the Nader study will have justified itself. But it also has, for the first time, cataloged most of the state's land use ills, and despite charges that it is mostly a rehash, it contains a large mass of new material. Whether the conditions are new matters little; the central issue is that they still *exist* and continue to operate against the public interest and that relatively little has been done to correct them.

Nader's charges have not been successfully refuted. In assessing his report or any documented piece of muckraking critics would serve the public better by dwelling more on the gravity of the conditions that are attacked and less on tone, bias, or minor shortcomings of the presentation.

The Nader report was researched and written by 25 of "Nader's Raiders," the largest such task force ever assembled by the consumer advocate for a single study project. The group included two economists, a city planner, a biologist, and several lawyers. More than half of them are or have been California residents. The study took 15 months to complete; the charge that it was a "shoddy product" simply doesn't stand up.

14

What Must Be Done

Iᴛ has been many years since deleterious land subdividing and selling gave rise to serious national concern, yet the situation today is more alarming than ever. Moreover, the potential for further damage is ominous. The need for reforms has been made ever more critical by the nation's burgeoning growth. As the *Washington Post* noted in a 1971 editorial:

> Between now and the end of this century, the statisticians say, we will build as much again as we have built in our entire history. We will build a second America, as it were. Every 10 years new homes and apartment houses, schools and hospitals, factories and offices, roads and railroads, shops and parking lots, gas stations and whatever will cover some 5 million acres, an area the size of New Jersey. . . .And while it is true that the population as a whole may not increase quite as rapidly as predicted some years ago, the pace of urbanization is not likely to decrease because we keep using up more and more land per person. . . .Land, in short, is becoming our most precious commodity.

Obviously we can no longer afford to allow such a vital resource to be ravaged by greedy or irresponsible subdividers. The building of the "second America" must be entrusted to people who are willing and able to undertake quality development.

Fortunately the many people who recognize this are succeeding more and more in making themselves heard, and momentum for reform is growing. Legislation is pending in Congress that would, for the first time, establish a national land use policy. Land use controls have been enacted in a few states already, and reform proposals have been introduced in others.

The Federal Trade Commission, which has broad powers to protect the public from unfair business practices, is investigating land selling practices in depth. Consumer-protection groups have become more cognizant of the insidious deceptions in many land offerings and are warning the public about them. Environmentalists, who wield tremendous clout today, have joined the battle in many areas. Consumer organizations are rallying behind legislation in Congress that would establish an independent federal government office to protect the interests of all consumers. Another bill would make it much easier for victimized consumers to institute class-action lawsuits against merchants and corporations. Still another bill would abolish the Office of Interstate Land Sales Registration and replace it with a federal real estate commission whose members would be appointed by the president.

As one might imagine, an amalgamation of special interests is mobilizing to fight proposals that might restrict their operations. As the *New York Times* once said, "Every time any unit of government acts to protect the land, it finds itself in an expensive race with the speculators."

In the months and years ahead we will probably witness any number of ferocious confrontations between environmentalists and consumer-protection agencies on one hand and land owners and real estate forces on the other. The outcome of such fights could have a significant impact on the quality of life for many Americans in years to come. "The responses we make to conditions that exist today are of monumental importance to

212 THE GREAT LAND HUSTLE

the land ethics we bequeath to future generations," declares
Secretary of the Interior Morton. Senator Henry M. Jackson
(D-Wash.), sponsor of one of the land use bills in Congress,
said: "The problems of the present look relatively insignificant
when they are compared with the problems we will have in
10, 20, 30 years *if* we accept supinely the ultimate consequences
of some current projections of future requirements."

The formulation of an effective land use policy entails much
more, of course, than the regulation of subdividers, but this is
a major element of such a program. To deal effectively with the
problems set forth in this book a combination of land use
controls and consumer-protection measures is necessary.
Before the approaches that have been tried and recommended
are examined, the objectives of a comprehensive reform program should be stated. Precisely what must be accomplished?

The chief aims should be:

(1) to curb, as much as possible, the creation of premature,
unneeded, and substandard subdivisions;

(2) to establish reasonable standards of quality for all new
subdivisions;

(3) to protect buyers of subdivided land from unfair offerings
and practices, and

(4) to restrict severely the selling of lots as speculative
investments.

How can these things be accomplished? Through the years
I have discussed that question with scores of land planners,
investment counsellors, and real estate authorities. While there
has been a certain amount of disagreement over details, there
has been surprising unanimity over what basic tools are needed.
They are:

(1) stringent disclosure requirements at the federal level for
most subdivision offerings involved in interstate commerce;

(2) strict censorship of advertising;

(3) strong subdivision controls at the state and county levels;
and

(4) a federal agency the sole mission of which would be the

defense of consumer interests, such as that proposed in Congress and staunchly supported by such groups as the Consumer Federation of America and the AFL-CIO.

Restricting sales of lots as speculative investments is one of the most debatable of the aims. Some critics contend that such selling should be prohibited because so many people are hurt by it, but prohibition is neither possible nor desirable. In certain circumstances lots *can* be a worthwhile investment. No regulatory machinery should stifle legitimate business or unfairly infringe on a landowner's ability to dispose of property. By the same token, the public should be protected from phony or dubious investment schemes of all kinds. The best method for doing this yet devised (aside from subdivision control, which will be discussed later) is the regulation of subdivision lots sold as investments in interstate commerce as *securities* — as eight states do now and as drafters of the federal land sales law originally proposed. Disclosure requirements should continue to be administered at the federal level — a profusion of state regulations could lead to utter chaos — but the responsibility should be shifted from the Department of Housing and Urban Development to the Securities and Exchange Commission or to an independent agency.

HUD's performance in regulating land sellers — prior to mid-1972, at least — qualifies as one of the greatest of bureaucratic boondoggles, but such a fiasco was to be expected. HUD is not a consumer-protection agency; its mission is to promote, encourage, and help to facilitate housing construction and community development. The agency is developer-oriented. Asking HUD to regulate developers is comparable to asking the Department of Commerce to administer antitrust laws. The function of the SEC, by contrast, is not to promote the securities business but to keep it as honest as possible, and while that agency may have certain failings, its accomplishments have been impressive.

There are many legal precedents for regulating subdivided land offerings as securities. Promotional lots sold on installment contracts closely resemble stock in a corporation in several respects. Buyers of such lots are really *bankers*, with a security interest in the developments. They are actually *financing* the developments with their contract payments, although they are *paying* interest instead of *getting* it, as they would if they loaned money to a corporation or to the federal government by buying bonds. The money from those monthly payments forms the cash flow that keeps the developer in business. The lot buyers put up most of the money and assume most of the risks, yet all they receive in return is a piece of paper on which the developer agrees to convey a piece of ground to them at a future time. There is no appreciable difference between a business venture that is financed with proceeds from sales of stock and a community development that is financed with proceeds from sales of lots.

If the financing of community developments from installment contracts on lots serves a useful purpose and is in the public interest, such undertakings should have no difficulty complying with the securities laws. If people want to help to finance a development by buying a lot, they should be allowed to do so, just as they are allowed to buy stock in a business venture. But buyers should be made aware of exactly what they are getting into, just as securities buyers are informed of their negotiations; a land sales prospectus should resemble a securities prospectus. It should contain every particle of information that relates to the offering, including an appraisal of its current value and a listing of factors that could affect its *future* value. If the subdividers could continue to stake out more lots and put them up for sale, the prospectus should explain that this could *dilute* the value of lots presently held. If a buyer could encounter difficulties in attempting to sell a lot, that fact should be made clear. If the developer has not made adequate financial arrangements to guarantee promised improvements, that fact and its consequences should be heavily underscored.

All restrictions, caveats, adverse information, and uncertainties relating to an offering and the company should be listed in the prospectus under the category of *risk factors*.

The more salient of these should appear on the cover in boldface type, as is done in a securities prospectus.

Meaningful disclosure would help to protect buyers and would be a strong deterrent to dishonest or unfair offerings. If the whole truth about a subdivision were made available in writing to every potential customer, the subdivider would do a lot of thinking before investing his time, money, and energy in a questionable scheme.

Because of the high pressure and gimmickry that are so common in land sales, the disclosure law should also provide a *cooling-off period* of at least 48 hours, during which purchasers could cancel a contract for any reason. It would certainly be in the public interest to allow land buyers sufficient time to investigate an offer properly and to ascertain whether it was truthfully presented.

But disclosure alone is not enough. Some people will be fooled no matter how much they are told, and many others will continue to have mistaken notions about the investment potential of subdivided land. As long as that is the case, undesirable subdividing and selling practices will persist, and *subdivision control* will be necessary.

State and local governments should regulate land subdividers as strictly as they regulate banks, insurance companies, liquor stores, and other types of business. Each state should have a subdivision control board to prescribe standards for subdivisions and limit their number, just as banks, insurance companies, and other enterprises are limited.

All new subdivisions should be required to have such basic improvements as adequate drainage and road access. If septic tanks might cause a health hazard, sewage systems should be required. Reasonable standards of quality should be established for all grading, paving, and other improvements. Subdividers should be required to post bonds or to provide equivalent financial security to guarantee that any promised improvements would actually be provided.

Builders of subdivisions in urban areas are commonly required to post surety bonds. That requirement should be imposed on nearly *all* subdividers. In some cases, however, it might be more practical to require the subdivider to place a percentage of the proceeds from each lot sale into a trust fund or escrow account from which funds for improvements would be drawn.

In licensing subdivision offerings states should apply the fairness principle that is used by California in regulating subdivision offerings and by most states in regulating securities sales. Most states won't let a promoter sell stock in worthless schemes, even if investors are told that the scheme is worthless. Some state laws bar securities transactions that state officials consider unfair to investors in any way. For example, California requires an applicant for a permit to issue securities that will be sold in the state to show that "The proposed plan of business of the applicant and the proposed issuance of securities are fair, just and equitable, and that the applicant intends to transact its business fairly and honestly."

New Hampshire can prohibit the sale of stock if it determines that the securities are "of such a character that there is a serious financial danger to the purchaser in buying them."* Why not apply similar rules to real estate? Such measures would accomplish two things: they would make premature subdividing economically unsound in many or most cases; they would help assure that the subdivisions that *are* platted would be of sufficient quality not to fall into disrepair and have to be maintained with public funds.

It will be argued by developers, of course, that those kinds of restrictions would interfere with a landowner's ability to sell his property. There would, perhaps, be interference in some cases, but the protection of society must come first. The "pioneer land ethic," which holds that the owner of land "has the God-given right to do with it as he damned pleases,"

---

* State securities regulations are widely referred to as "blue sky laws." That term was first applied to rules governing subdivision promotions. The securities laws of most states are patterned after the blue sky law that Kansas adopted in 1911. It was given its name because it was enacted to enable the state to crack down on promoters who "would sell building lots in the blue sky."

has no validity and should be given no credence. For more than a half-century governments have used their zoning authority to control land use. Most jurisdictions, for instance, prohibit construction of incinerators next to country clubs. They should also prohibit (as many do now) the subdividing of land in ways that create burdens for other people.

In addition to these measures the FTC should require subdivision advertisers to substantiate their claims, as it does with many other advertisers. If a subdivider promotes property as a potentially profitable investment, he should be made to submit convincing evidence that such representations are justified. Land sellers should be permitted to make reasonable value judgments, but those that are patently fraudulent or exaggerated should be banned.

To sum up, then, we need an SEC-type federal agency to enforce disclosure requirements, state or local laws and agencies to control the subdividing of land, and better advertising supervision. Unfortunately, while drafting good legislation is relatively simple, passing it and making it work are usually far more difficult matters.

In Washington, D.C., and in every state capital are corps of lobbyists and special interest groups involved directly or indirectly in real estate — developers, builders, brokers, title companies, contractors, and lawyers — who are not likely to be disposed kindly toward laws that could hurt their business. We have seen how the federal law was weakened and how reform proposals were torpedoed in New Mexico. The same thing happened this year in Arizona, a state where, in the opinion of state planning director Harry Higgins, at least half of the estimated 500,000 acres of rural subdivision offerings are "of the snakeoil variety."

Recently developer interests in California, where subdivisions cover much of the coastline, scored a major victory when a state Senate committee killed four conservation bills that would have transferred control of coastal development from local communities to the state. Proponents of the measures maintained that much despoilation takes place because local governments frequently ignore abuses by developers. A study by the University of California concurred, commenting: "It is an unhappy fact of life that local governments, in their quest for tax revenues, frequently become allied with forces of economic exploitation that may be hostile to preserving and enhancing the natural coastal environment."

Ralph Nader was more blunt about it. Developers and other commercial interests "to a significant extent have bought, intimidated, compromised, and supplied key officials in state and local government to a point where these interests govern the governed," charged his report on power and land in California.

None of this should be cause for despair, however. On the whole, the outlook over the country is anything but bleak. Prospects for enactment of long-needed land use controls were probably never brighter. Interest in ecology and environmental forces have won important skirmishes with developers in recent years, and they will do so again.

By 1972 ten states — Colorado, Delaware, Hawaii, Maine, Massachusetts, Michigan, New York, Oregon, Vermont, and Wisconsin — had adopted some form of state control over land use. Delaware pioneered legislation in 1971 by banning all new heavy industry from its coastline and requiring existing industries in those areas to obtain state permission for any expansion.

Pressure for better land use and subdivision regulations has been growing in several other states, including Pennsylvania, Arizona, Minnesota, and Michigan.

In Washington support is growing for legislation that would commit the nation to a land use policy aimed at protecting land, rivers, streams, estuaries, coastal zones, and other irreplaceable resources. Of approximately 120 land use policy bills that have been introduced, two are currently under final consideration by the Senate Committee on Interior and Insular Affairs.* One measure (S.632) is sponsored by Wash-

* It appears likely that Congress will vote on one or both of the measures this year.

ington's Senator Jackson, and the other (S.992) is included in a package of environmental legislation introduced by the Nixon administration.

Both bills would encourage the states to develop and implement statewide land use plans, which would be subject to federal review to assure coordination. The bills provide for partial financing of the programs with federal funds. Federal activities involving the use of land, such as construction of highways, parks, and dams, would be coordinated with state plans.

There is a major difference between the two proposals, however. Jackson's bill would require *comprehensive statewide planning* by the states, while the administration's bill calls for state control only over lands in "special areas" or on which "special uses" might be located. "The requirement of comprehensiveness would ensure a broad and careful consideration and integration of all relevant social, economic, and environmental concerns," Senator Jackson explained. "To further ensure careful long-range planning my measure contains a 'balanced' set of economic, social, and environmental criteria of which the states must take cognizance in developing their plans. The criteria do not say 'thou shalt have so much of this and so much of that.' Rather, they merely say to the states they must not fail to consider, and attempt to develop, their *own* integrative solutions to the full range of their citizens' varied needs: environmental, recreational, service, energy, industrial, house, and transportation."

Since comprehensive planning is essential, the Jackson version appears infinitely superior to the Nixon plan.

A bill that purports to deal with fraudulent and deceptive land sales has been introduced by U.S. Representative Barry Goldwater, Jr. of Arizona. Called the Real Estate and Securities Act of 1972, the measure would establish a national real estate commission the five members of which would be appointed by the president. The sole concern of the commission would be the regulation of real estate and real estate securities sold in interstate commerce. The act "would require complete and full disclosure of all facts and a determination that no fraud is being perpetrated before the offering can be made to the public," declared Goldwater.

Although this plan offers a distinct improvement over the OILSR program, it does not specifically provide for the classification of subdivision offerings as securities, and it seems to be considerably weaker than the California law that stipulates that such offerings must be certified as fair, just, and equitable. Goldwater was elected in 1970 from California's 27th Congressional district, which includes California City and many other promotional subdivisions. His people say that Goldwater's bill was prompted by concern over such activities; skeptics fear that it may be an attempt to head off tougher measures.

The concept of a national real estate commission seems salubrious indeed, but reform seekers should make a thorough examination of the Goldwater bill and all other reform proposals. As we have seen, there has been a long procession of laws, boards, and agencies that were created to stamp out wrongs, but they failed because they were not adequately implemented or funded, because they were infiltrated by the people they were supposed to police, or because their personnel lacked the expertise to carry out their assignments effectively. Such disasters can make the problem of land sales abuses worse than before. One of the greatest disservices a government can do is to enact protective legislation but fail to enforce it properly. The public, thinking that it is safeguarded by law, becomes more vulnerable than ever to swindlers and con artists.

Besides being watchful for phony solutions, reform advocates must be prepared for frustrating setbacks. Righting wrongs often takes years, even decades.

The trouncing that environmentalists suffered in California was not a total calamity. Uncertainties created by controversy over the conservation bills slowed the tide of development, at least temporarily. "I personally know of $270 million in projects that have been canceled simply because of gas from the ecologists," growled J. Jamison Moore, a management consultant who opposed the bills.

Reform seekers in Arizona, like those in New Mexico, have vowed to fight on. When subdivision-control bills died in the Arizona legislature this year, advocates launched a campaign to force the enactment of stricter regulations through the initiative process. A statewide drive for initiative-petition signatures was organized by the newly-formed Coalition of Environmental Groups of Tucson.

The laws that protect us from contaminated food and drugs, hazardous products, financial manipulators, shaky banks, avaricious money-lenders, and a host of other perils were passed only after years of bitter struggle. It took more than ten acrimonious years just to put the truth-in-lending law on the books, but it finally got there in 1968 despite the fierce opposition of bankers, finance companies, merchants, car dealers, lawyers, the American Retail Federation, and the U.S. Chamber of Commerce.

Preparation, organization, and strategy are important in pushing for new land sales and subdivision laws. Proponents should know exactly what they want and why. They should muster all the strength they can; consumerists should join forces with environmentalists, conservationists, and planners. They should arm themselves with incontrovertible proof that premature and poor quality subdividing endangers the public interest and be able to show *where* and *how* it does so. Examples must be presented of development projects that have gone sour; of platted acreage that is idle and unproductive; of development practices that damage the environment by causing erosion, scarring of the landscape, or pollution; of wasteful subdividing practices; of people who have been defrauded by land hustlers.

Reformers should try to convince voters, legislators, and builders that sensible rules will *not* jeopardize legitimate and necessary development; that premature subdividing is *not* in the public interest; that subdivisions that owe their existence to deceptive selling serve only to enrich scoundrels who use the proceeds to launch new nefarious schemes or to pay off corrupt public officials.

A major obstacle to attainment of effective subdivision

policies is the belief of many officials, especially county commissioners in thinly developed regions, that almost any scheme that may attract people to the area is desirable. Local officials are responsible for zoning and land use planning in most places where such functions exist, and they are seldom willing to relinquish such authority. However, basic planning decisions usually are best made at the state level, where officials are more visible and less vulnerable to pressures and blandishments from subdividers than are county officials.

A novel battle plan was used in Colorado to deal with this problem, and it provides a useful blueprint for other states. The land fever is high in Colorado (the Rocky Mountain Center on Environment estimated in 1971 that bulldozers were carving up at least 1 million acres for subdivisions). Already critical problems are evident. On some of the steep slopes of the Rockies, where innumerable "view location" homesites have been sold, raw sewage trickles downhill because septic tanks do not work properly in the high-density soil. Danger from fire is heightened by remoteness, heavy vegetation, and scarcity of water. Erosion is a menace. The pace of growth has caused such uneasiness among residents that the Colorado Institute on Population Problems recently adopted the slogan: "Think Small!"

In 1970 Governor John Love appointed a seven-member commission to develop a statewide land use program. Its recommendations, drafted after nine months of study, resulted in the writing of a statewide Land Use Act, which was subsequently adopted by the legislature.

The act required that each of the state's 63 counties establish a planning board to draft rules — based on the state's guidelines — for the platting of new subdivisions.

Fearing the worst, farmers, ranchers, and assorted real estate interests joined in an attempt to kill the program. But the land use commission outflanked them by holding a series of about 30 workshop sessions around the state and inviting all interested parties to attend. Once the plan was explained in detail, much of the opposition relented. In the end the commission had compiled an inventory of Colorado's natural resources and had won broad support for its objectives. The counties continue to call the shots on land use, but now they must adhere to state policy. The law was strengthened further in 1972.

And, to the surprise and delight of reformers, subdivision-control legislation was also approved in that stronghold of land hustlers, Florida. A package of bills spearheaded by a young (43) and popular reform governor, Reubin O. Askew, cleared the legislature this year despite stiff opposition from home builders and many developers. Florida's new program, like Colorado's, leaves responsibility for approving subdivision plats largely with local agencies, but decisions affecting developments having regional impact can now be appealed to a new body, the State Land and Water Adjudicatory Board composed of the governor and members of his cabinet. Also, the state can now designate areas of critical environmental concern and exercise regulatory authority within them.

"This is definitely the greatest step forward that Florida has ever taken in the environmental area," rejoiced Joy Landers, an Askew aide. Whether the plan is really that propitious remains to be seen, but at least a start has been made.

Previously, the federal government killed two multimillion-dollar projects in Florida, a huge jet airport west of Miami and a 107-mile barge canal that would have provided a water route between Jacksonville and the Gulf Coast. Both undertakings were warmly supported by certain business interests, but after a long uphill battle, conservationists finally convinced Washington that they would inflict irreparable damage to Florida's fragile ecosystems.

And U.S. Senator Lawton M. Chiles of Florida introduced a bill in Congress under which the federal government would purchase 547,000 acres of Big Cypress Swamp, which adjoins the Everglades, and would preserve the land as a national recreation area. The Nixon administration subsequently announced its intention to sponsor a similar measure.

In Florida, Colorado, and elsewhere, unprincipled land

hustlers can and should be halted once and for all. The selling of land on a national and international scale is a relatively new phenomenon, and it is still largely unregulated. There comes a time in the evolution of nearly every business and profession when rules of conduct must be prescribed and enforced. Some of our most respected occupations underwent periods of rampant misbehavior during their formative years: medicine had great numbers of quacks; insurance, underfinanced companies; the securities business, bucket shops; before the passage of food and drug laws the selling of tainted meat was not uncommon; before governments began to regulate them, some banks toppled with every economic contraction. It is time now for the land hustlers to go through the same evolutionary process.

Taming the land hustlers will take time, effort, skill, imagination, organization, and patience. Subdividing land is still one of the quickest and easiest ways of making a fast buck, and its proponents have a lot to fight for. But the price of continued procrastination is much too high to pay.

Appendix

Listed below are the principal regulatory agencies and other organizations from which authorative information relating to subdivided land offerings can be obtained, usually without charge:

Bureau of the Census, Washington, D.C. 20233. The bureau will supply population figures and projections for all sections of the country. It also publishes useful data on farm acreage prices and on the number of vacant lots in each state.

Council of Better Business Bureaus, Inc., 1150 Seventeenth Street NW, Washington, D.C. 20036. A national organization of local better business bureaus, the council has issued detailed reports on some land companies and has compiled material on several others. The reports are available from local bureaus as well as from the national office.

Department of Justice, Constitution Avenue and Tenth Street

NW, Washington, D.C. 20530. If a company has been convicted of violating federal law, the department will have a record of it.

Federal Trade Commission, Pennsylvania Avenue and Sixth Street NW, Washington, D.C. 20580. The FTC has collected considerable information on some of the leading land firms.

Office of Interstate Land Sales Registration, Department of Housing and Urban Development, 451 Seventh Street SW, Washington, D.C. 20410. The OILSR has extensive data on thousands of land offerings and, for $2.50 a copy, will furnish property reports for specific subdivisions.

U.S. Postal Service, Twelfth Street and Pennsylvania Avenue NW, Washington, D.C. 20260. Postal officials can advise whether a company has been found in violation of mail-fraud laws or other postal regulations.

The following state agencies have varying degrees of jurisdiction over sales of subdivided land and of sales personnel.

Alabama — Alabama Real Estate Commission, 526 State Office Building, Montgomery, Alabama 36104.

Alaska — Division of Banking, Securities, Small Loans and Corporations, Department of Commerce, Pouch D, Juneau, Alaska 99801.

Arizona — State of Arizona Real Estate Department, 2801 N. Fifteenth Avenue, Phoenix, Arizona 85007.

Arkansas — Arkansas Real Estate Commission, 1311 W. Second St., Little Rock, Arkansas 72201.

California — Commissioner, California Department of Real Estate, 714 P Street, Sacramento, California 95814.

Colorado — Colorado Real Estate Commission, 110 State Services Building, Denver, Colorado 80203.

Connecticut — State of Connecticut Real Estate Commission, 90 Washington Street, Hartford, Connecticut 06115.

Delaware — Delaware Real Estate Commission, Old State House, Dover, Delaware 19901.

District of Columbia — Government of the District of Columbia, 614 H Street NW, Room 107, Washington, D.C. 20001.

Florida — State of Florida Department of Business Regulation, Division of Florida Land Sales, 2942 W. Columbus Drive, Tampa, Florida 33607.

Georgia — Georgia Real Estate Commission, 166 Pryor Street SW, Atlanta, Georgia 30303.

Hawaii — State of Hawaii Professional and Vocational Licensing Division, Department of Regulatory Agencies, Post Office Box 3469, Honolulu, Hawaii 96801.

Idaho — Idaho State Real Estate Commission, 517 N. Third Street, Boise, Idaho 83702.

Illinois — State of Illinois Department of Registration and Education, Springfield, Illinois 62706.

Indiana — State of Indiana Real Estate Commission, Indianapolis, Indiana 46204.

Iowa — State of Iowa Real Estate Commission, State Capitol, Des Moines, Iowa 50319.

Kansas — Office of the Securities Commission, State Office Building, Topeka, Kansas 66612.

Kentucky — Kentucky State Real Estate Commission, Suite 610, Republic Building, Fifth and Walnut, Louisville, Kentucky 40202.

Louisiana — Louisiana Real Estate Commission, State Capitol, Baton Rouge, Louisiana 70804.

Maine — Department of Banks and Banking, Securities Division, Augusta, Maine 04330.

Maryland — Maryland Real Estate Commission, 1 Calvert Street, Baltimore, Maryland 21201.

Massachusetts — The Commonwealth of Massachusetts, Division of Registration, Board of Registration of Real Estate, Leverett Saltonstall Building, 100 Cambridge Street, Boston, Massachusetts 02202.

Michigan — Department of Licensing and Regulation, 1033 S. Washington Avenue, Lansing, Michigan 48926.

Minnesota — State of Minnesota, Division of Securities, Real Estate Section, 260 State Office Building, St. Paul, Minnesota 55102.

Mississippi — Mississippi Real Estate Commission, 505 Woodland Hills Building, 3000 Old Canton Road, Jackson, Mississippi 39216.

Missouri — Securities Division, Office of Secretary of State, Capitol Building, Jefferson City, Missouri 65101.

Montana — Montana Real Estate Commission, 504 Lamborn Street, Helena, Montana 59601.

Nebraska — Nebraska Real Estate Commission, State Capitol, Lincoln, Nebraska 68509.

Nevada — Department of Commerce, Real Estate Division, Room 315, Nye Building, 201 S. Fall Street, Carson City, Nevada 89701.

New Hampshire — Consumer Protection Division, State of New Hampshire, State House Annex, Concord, New Hampshire 03301.

New Jersey — State of New Jersey, Division of Real Estate, Trenton, New Jersey 08265.

New Mexico — Director of Land Subdivisions, Office of the Attorney General, P.O. Box 2246, Santa Fe, New Mexico 87501; New Mexico Real Estate Commission, Room 1031, 505 Marquette NW, Albuquerque, New Mexico 87101.

New York — Deputy Secretary of State, General Counsel, Department of State, 270 Broadway, New York, New York 10007.

North Carolina — North Carolina Real Estate Licensing Board, P.O. Box 266, Raleigh, North Carolina 27602.

North Dakota — North Dakota Real Estate Commission, P.O. Box 727, 410 E. Thayer Avenue, Bismarck, North Dakota 58501.

Ohio — Commissioner of Securities, 366 E. Broad Street,

Columbus, Ohio 43215; State Real Estate Commission, 366 E. Broad Street, Columbus, Ohio 43215.

Oklahoma — Oklahoma Real Estate Commission, 315 Will Rogers Memorial Building, Oklahoma City, Oklahoma 73105.

Oregon — Real Estate Division, Commerce Building, Salem, Oregon 97310.

Pennsylvania — Office of the Attorney General, Bureau of Consumer Protection, 2-4 N. Market Square, Harrisburg, Pennsylvania 17101; Pennsylvania Real Estate Commission, P.O. Box 2649, Harrisburg, Pennsylvania 17101.

Rhode Island — Real Estate Division, State of Rhode Island, 169 Weybasset Street, Providence, Rhode Island 02903.

South Carolina — South Carolina Real Estate Board, P.O. Box 11396, 502 Columbia Building, Columbia, South Carolina 29211.

South Dakota — South Dakota Real Estate Commission, 319 S. Coteau, P.O. Box 638, Pierre, South Dakota 57501.

Tennessee — Department of Insurance, Division of Securities, State Office Building, Room 114, Nashville, Tennessee 37201.

Texas — Texas Real Estate Commission, P.O. Box 12188, Capital Station, Austin, Texas 78711.

Utah — State of Utah Department of Business Regulation, Division of Real Estate, 330 E. Fourth Street S., Salt Lake City, Utah 84111.

Vermont — Department of Banking and Insurance, Division of Banking, Montpelier, Vermont 05602.

Virginia — Virginia Real Estate Commission, P.O. Box 1-X, Richmond, Virginia 23202.

Virgin Islands — Virgin Islands Real Estate Commission, St. Thomas, Virgin Islands 00801; United States Attorney, District Court Building, Charlotte Amalie, St. Thomas, Virgin Islands 00801.

Washington — Administrator of Securities, Department of

Licenses, Security Division, P.O. Box 648, Olympia, Washington.

West Virginia — Deputy Securities Commissioner, State Auditor's Office, Charleston, West Virginia 25305.

Wisconsin — Wisconsin Real Estate Examining Board, 819 North Sixth Street, Milwaukee, Wisconsin 53203.

Wyoming — Wyoming Real Estate Commission, 313 Capital Building, Cheyenne, Wyoming 82001.

Index

L

M

Minuit, Peter, 108
Mondale, Walter F., 119, 171
"money-back" guarantee,
    123, 124
Montague, H. B., 111
Moore, J. Jamison, 220
Morton, Rogers, 80, 212
Moss, Frank E., 182, 201
Mountain View Homes, Inc.,
    89
Mudd, Harvey, 192-194, 196
Murphy, Thomas J., 181

N

Nader, Ralph, 181
    task force report: *see*
    California, Power and
    Land in,
National Association of Home
    Builders (NAHB), 85, 92,
    104, 171
National Association of Real
    Estate Boards, 131, 165,
    193
National Better Business
    Bureau, Inc. (NBBB), 159,
    161
National Housing Center
    Council, 85
National Land Council, Inc.,
    184, 185
Nevada County, 78
New Babylon, Kansas, 64
New Mexico, case study,
    189-197
New Smyrna Acres, Florida,
    113
"new town," 73

New York, state regulatory
    program, 119, 120, 168,169
Nixon, Richard, 82, 181-184,
    219
Nortek, Inc., 118, 119, 181
Nova Industrial Park, Florida,
    8, 113

O

Ocean View Estates, Hawaii,
    117
Office of Interstate Land Sales
    Registration (OILSR),
    172-181
    Charnita, Pennsylvania,
        98, 100
    inspection trips, 125
    reform, 186, 187
    televised warnings, 61, 62
O'Leary, Gerald P., 52, 57
O'Leary, Harlan E., 52
Orange County Acres,
    Florida, 112, 113

P

Palm Coast, Florida, 30-43,
    74, 203, 204
Paul, Ivan, 140, 141
Paulson, Morton C., 36-41,
    162, 164, 165
Perine, Thomas J., 86
Perman, Mr. and Mrs., 98, 99,
    175
Pew, Thomas W., 27
Phillips, John M., Jr., 57
Pilnik, Louis, 119

Due